Author's note

This true story of triumph over adversity can give hope and inspiration to many people, young and old, who are facing anxiety and hardship in these difficult times. It also provides the humour which is so essential to our lives during these periods.

I hope you enjoy it

Ray

***

More information about the author and his books including a series of short video clips can be found at the following social media sites.

Facebook: www.facebook.com/ray.saunders.author

Twitter: @author_saunders

Instagram: raysaunders_author

HOW LUCKY CAN YOU GET

Ray Saunders

HOW LUCKY CAN YOU GET

Vanguard Press

A CIP catalogue record for this title is
available from the British Library.

ISBN 978 1 78465 735 2

Vanguard Press is an imprint of
Pegasus Elliot MacKenzie Publishers Ltd.
www.pegasuspublishers.com

First Published in 2020

Vanguard Press
Sheraton House Castle Park
Cambridge England

Printed & Bound in Great Britain

Dedication

To Jill

Acknowledgements

My thanks to my nephew, Grant Moody and his
partner, Richard Lavender for their help and
encouragement for me to write this book.

Chapter 1

I heard the roar of its engines as the German bomber swept low over the railway embankment. Then came a loud whoosh followed by an ear-splitting explosion. The first bomb demolished the end house of the row of terraced houses where we lived.

I ran out from the garden shed where I was playing, as the second bomb exploded in the field opposite, sending up large clods of clay soil about eighty yards away. As the third bomb hit a tobacconist shop in the high street, I saw the Messerschmitt climb away into the sky.

I ran up the garden path towards our house, to be met by my mother who was running down to see if I was all right. The neighbours all came out chattering about what had happened. No one had been hurt, as the people in the end house were out shopping. We then all went around over the river bridge to the field and we inspected the large crater.

I still recall the strong smell of what seemed to me to be gas but it was probably the burnt explosive. The other children and I collected small pieces of the bomb casing for souvenirs, which were jagged and still hot.

It was the first year of the Second World War and I was ten years old.

On the third of September 1939, sixteen days before my tenth birthday, the Prime Minister Neville Chamberlain, at eleven a.m. broadcast to the nation. My father was sitting beside the radio and I stood there beside my mother. I remember his words:

"This morning the British Ambassador in Berlin handed the German Government a final note, stating that unless we heard from them by eleven o'clock, that they were prepared at once to withdraw their troops from Poland, a state of war would exist between us. I have to tell you now that no such undertaking has been received, and that consequently, this country is at war with Germany."

All the air raid sirens started wailing and I turned to my mother and I said, "Mummy will we all be killed?"

We had already been issued with gas masks, as a gas attack was thought likely. I hated the smell of the rubber and I did not know then that the air filter that screwed onto the front, was filled with asbestos.

These masks came in small cardboard boxes with a shoulder sling made of string, and you were supposed to take them with you at all times.

The following May, Chamberlain resigned, and Winston Churchill became Prime Minister and he formed a new Coalition Government and War Cabinet

The old terraced houses where we lived were built six to a row, with passages between each block. They were just two up and two down and they had a brick-built scullery, with a brick floor laid on sand. Attached to this was a brick outside lavatory with a WC pan set into the floor, and a high-level cast-iron cistern.

Both buildings had slate roofs that were visible from the inside. The lavatory door was wooden with a six-inch gap top and bottom. On the inside was a nail that was used to hang old newspapers on that we used as toilet paper.

In the corner of the scullery there was a brick 'copper' lined with cement. It formed a bowl to hold water and had a wooden lid. There was a 'copper stick' that was used to 'stodge' the washing. Underneath was a grate for a wood fire to boil the water.

Our scullery had a large gas stove and a big old iron mangle along one side, opposite the back door. Along the other side was an old stone sink on brick plinths. There was only one tap over the sink, and all the pipes were made of lead which froze up every winter.

There was an old wooden draining board that my mother had covered with linoleum, the edges of which had curled up to reveal a deposit of black gunge.

On the wall was a metal box with a small wire mesh door, in which food was kept keeping the flies off. A mirror hung from a nail on the brick wall to the left side of the sink, and to the right was a small rectangular window.

When my mother used the mangle, I was fascinated to see the water being squeezed out of the clothes and then running down the wooden tray to the small galvanised bath beneath.

One day whilst playing, I noticed a packet of lard on the side of the gas stove and I wondered what it would do if I mangled it.

The result was a horrible mess and I ran to my mother saying, "Mummy I don't know how it got there."

She then had to dismantle the wooden rollers to try and clean it off. Despite this she didn't punish me and she laughed as she saw the funny side of it.

Below the scullery roof was a large beam with a row of four-inch nails that we hung things from. At Christmas there would be dead rabbits waiting to be skinned or perhaps a pheasant or two that had been poached.

As a child, I lived in this house with my father, my mother and her parents. We kept rabbits and we bred them for food. When it came time to kill them, this was done by my mother or by my grandfather as my father couldn't bring himself to do it.

My grandmother, who I always called Gran, had a sister 'Fan' who lived with her husband on a farm in Hadlow, where her husband worked.

Their son George lived with them. Uncle George was a poacher and one moonlit night, he persuaded my father to go with him into the woods to get some pheasants.

Spotting one roosting in a tree, he gave my father the gun and told him to shoot it, while he watched out for the keeper.

My father said that when he pulled the trigger there was an explosion loud enough to wake up the whole village, and when the pheasant hit the ground it didn't have a feather on it.

Some nights we would all creep out into the fields with sacks and we pulled up the parsnips and cabbages. We also stole potatoes from the straw 'clamps' where they were stored for the winter.

Afterwards, we would go back to Aunt Fan's and have hot broth and the men would drink her home-made wine.

This was the early thirties and poorer families had to resort to this in order to live. There was no social security in those days. People nowadays in this country don't know what real poverty is.

The two small bedrooms in our house were used by my parents and my grandparents. There was no toilet or bathroom. We used enamel 'poes' that were kept under the bed. These had to be taken down and emptied if they had been used in the night.

I remember that mine had a brown 'crust' on the bottom that would sometimes flake off. It makes me wonder about the state of my kidneys, if my urine was producing this.

There was no form of heating, and in winter the windows would freeze on the inside. The only lighting for the bedrooms were candles that were carried upstairs fixed in enamel trays.

Some years later electricity was installed that enabled us to have electric lighting. This was provided by single wires that ran through metal pipes fixed to the walls.

The downstairs back room had two cupboards that were formed by a wooden partition that ran along under the stairs. One of these cupboards was used as the 'coal hole' where the coal was kept. The other was the 'food cupboard'. On the shelves would be all our food.

Mice would often leave their droppings on the breadboard and nibble the cheese. Traps were set up to catch them, and while sitting in the kitchen I would often hear them 'snap'.

Under the shelves was the gas meter, that had a slot where coins were inserted to buy a shilling's worth of gas. Every so often, the gasman would come and empty the container onto the kitchen table and count the shillings. I don't know how it worked, but my mother was always pleased when he checked his book and he then gave her a few shillings back. There was also a similar arrangement when the electricity was put in.

On the wall opposite was a kitchen range in front of which was a large wire fire guard, and in the hearth were two flat irons that my mother used by heating them on the range. She would do the ironing on the kitchen table. Above was a wooden mantlepiece to which my mother had fixed a strip of material, with drawing pins, to form a pelmet.

She used to thread her sewing and darning needles through this. When you needed to use one, you first had to use another one to clear the slot for the cotton. The reason for this was because my father would use them to dig his ears out. This meant that the slot became clogged up with dried earwax.

My mother had a hand operated Jones sewing machine and she was a self-taught seamstress. She made all my clothes, as well as her own, and she took in sewing. She would sit at one end of the kitchen table sewing.

One day the boy from next door asked if he could have a go. When he did, he turned to my mother and said, "When I turn the handle it makes my winkle go up and down."

We had a dartboard that hung on the door into the front room. We could not afford a proper one, so Dusty (Mum's father Henry Rhodes was always known as Dusty) made one from a large piece of elm. It was very hard, and the darts wouldn't stick, unless it was first soaked in water to soften it. Darts then were very light, made of wood with a metal tip at one end and a feather flight at the other. When they hit a wire, they would fly off in all directions. If they dropped onto the floor, they made little holes in the lino.

One evening, when Dad and Dusty were playing, a dart flew off. Mum was sitting at the table sewing and it stuck straight into the top of her head. We all laughed as she pulled it out and carried on sewing.

When the dartboard was taken off the door, it left a circle with little holes peppered all around it where the darts had missed.

We also had a shove-ha'penny board that Dad had made from a mahogany tabletop, that he'd taken from the hotel where he worked. We all played, and I remember that to make it slippery, it would be rubbed with old newspapers dipped in paraffin.

I had two table tennis bats, and a net that we'd fix to each side of the kitchen table. We would push back the chairs in order to play, and we usually finished up just bashing the ball back and forth at each other.

In the kitchen, there was a metal plate across the open chimney with a pipe connected to the range. The coal fires produced a lot of sooty tar that my mother would clean and sweep the chimney. She would then polish the range with blacking until it shone. Once a week she would bring in the old galvanised bath, that hung from a nail on the wall outside the back door. This was placed in front of the fireplace and then she would boil saucepans of water and fill it for my bath.

On each side of the mantlepiece were gas brackets that swivelled. Each had a glass globe and inside were small gas mantles. These were little cotton bags attached to chalky white rings that fitted over the gas pipe. When the gas was turned on, and a lighted match was held underneath, they would go 'pop' and light up. This would cause them to form a cobweb-like bulb that was very brittle. If you weren't careful the match could easily make a hole in them. They would then have to be replaced but they only cost a few pence.

The recess to the left of the chimney breast was covered with a curtain to hide the shelves. Our clothes were kept there, and on the floor beneath would be our shoes. It wasn't unusual to go for your shoes and find a half chewed dead rat, that our cat had brought in.

On the other side there was a recess with a table and on it stood an old battery powered radio. This was before we had electricity. The battery was a large, heavy accumulator. It was taken to a shop once a week to be recharged, and we were loaned another one. This cost sixpence (2½p).

On either side of the fireplace were two wooden armchairs with cushions. My mother's armchair was on the left and my father's, on the right. I wasn't allowed to sit in them and so I sat up at the table on one of the two wooden kitchen chairs.

There was a wire strung across the room, about one foot below the ceiling that Mum would use to dry the washing, when it was wet outside. She did all the decorating, and the wallpaper that she had covered the wooden panelling with, had a black mark along it, at shoulder height. This was caused by the coal man when he delivered the sacks of coal and tipped them into the 'coal hole' cupboard.

I think I was about four years old when my father's father, Mat Saunders, came to live with us. His second wife had died from cancer, and he was ill. He sat in a chair by the fireplace and he would cough up lumps of phlegm. He'd then open the range top and he would spit the phlegm into the fire. Sometimes he would miss, and it would hit the grate in front, where it would sizzle and burn to a crisp. When he died, he was placed in a coffin in our front room, where he lay until the funeral.

In the front room there was a three-piece suite, a sideboard and an open fireplace. This was only used for high days and holidays. On the sideboard was a large goldfish bowl where my solitary goldfish would swim around, waiting for its daily sprinkling of fish food.

Our front door opened onto the pavement, and across the road, there was a high wall that ran parallel to the railway embankment. It was the main line from the coast to London, and my mother would often complain on wash days, when the washing that she hung out to dry would get smothered in black smuts from the steam trains.

These trains continually ran up and down, carrying passengers and freight. She would scrub the stone threshold under the front door and apply a pumice stone to it that dried grey. She swept the pavement in front into the gutter. A road man would come down the road once a week with a pushcart, brush and shovel, to clean the street.

To say that these living conditions were Dickensian is no exaggeration.

This was my home, with little improvement, for the first twenty-five and a half years of my life, until I married, and Jill and I moved into a rented flat at the other end of the town.

Chapter 2

Ten years before World War Two started, I was born in the back bedroom of number 127, Vale Road, Tonbridge in Kent. It was just before the New York Stock Market crash and the beginning of the great depression that lasted for ten years.

It was a very difficult birth, attended by Nurse Turpin, the midwife, who my father nicknamed Dick. The doctor had to be called and he delivered me with forceps, the scars of which I carried on the back of my neck into manhood. My mother had to be cut and stitched as my head was too big to come through, and the top of my head hung over one ear. I weighed in at nine pounds.

The doctor told them that my scalp would grow back naturally, which it did. I'm not sure though if it caused some brain damage, as I had a difficult start and I can remember lying in her arms with my gaze fixed onto the top left corner of the bedroom. What I saw was a black hole from which came a terrifying throbbing noise.

My father said that I cried continuously for the first six months, during which time my mother was confined to bed. He would walk the room with me, and he would threaten to throw me out of the window, if I didn't stop crying. This was in the front bedroom, as they had exchanged bedrooms with my mother's parents who lived there with us.

My father had always been madly keen on football, and as a youth and a young man, he played for teams in Tunbridge Wells. He had a trial for a big club, but he was unable to follow his ambitions, and he must have felt trapped into a marriage all because of me.

I do not remember him ever hugging or kissing me. In all my life he had never ever told me that he loved me. I do not blame him for this as he had difficulty in showing emotion and he had many good points. He had never physically abused me. Sometimes, if I was cheeky, he would throw his slipper at me, but I soon learned to duck, and it developed my quick reflexes and my agility.

I was slow to begin talking, and when I did, I used words of my own. My word for a penny was 'guidey gar' and a sausage was an 'oomp nar'.

I was also left-handed. I started infant school aged five and I was found to be dyslexic. When I copied from the blackboard, I would write from right to left. There was no special provision for this condition in those days, and you often just sat at the back with crayons.

I remember that we sat on the wooden floor on raffia mats, and the teachers' name was Miss Moxam. My mother taught me to read phonetically from picture books, showing me the words for each subject. No one would have believed then, that in later life I would become a writer and a published author.

My mother was just twenty years old when she conceived me, and my father was two years older. Young people then were very immature, and they had almost no idea about contraception. They were made to marry by their parents, as having a child out of wedlock was very shameful.

I know nothing as to where or how I was conceived, or how they were married, as this was never discussed, and sex was a taboo subject. Had it been today she would probably have brought me up as a single parent, with state aid.

The three of us lived with her mother and father in the small house described above. Gran, as I called her, was a little round lady, rather strait-laced, although she had a good sense of humour. Having known real hardship in her upbringing, she was determined never to be without some money to fall back on. She was very thrifty, and as I grew older, she opened a Post Office savings account for me.

My grandfather, 'Dusty', was completely the opposite. He was outgoing and he loved nothing more than to play darts in the many pubs in the area. Tonbridge had thirty or so public houses at that time and also 'off licences'. These were private houses, where the front room was converted to form a small shop, that was licensed to sell beer and sometimes spirits and tobacco.

Most times he was happy-go-lucky, but one Sunday he came home drunk from the pub after they had closed at two p.m. and Gran 'carried on' at him. So, he picked up her dinner plate from the table and he threw it at the kitchen wall. It knocked a picture off its nail, and the chicken leg hung there with the gravy running down the wallpaper. He then sat down and ate his own.

Another time, when he had 'one too many', he was stopped by a man who stuttered, who tried to ask him the way.

Dusty said, "You, silly old bugger you've had too much sun."

However, this was unusual for him as he had a generous nature, and although he liked a drink, he never distressed our home because of it. My Gran was given most of his wages and she kept house. He always said that if it wasn't for her he'd be nothing.

Dusty always said, "A drunken man tells the truth."

I think this is true, and I'm always amused when a drunken politician says something, which he obviously believes, but then he apologises afterwards, denying that he meant it.

Some Sundays in summer, we would catch the train to Hastings and spend the day at the beach.

One Sunday we were waiting for Dusty who had gone to a pub in Vale Road called 'The Prince Albert'. The first talking pictures had just been made, and in 'The Jazz Singer', Al Jolson sang a song called 'Sonny Boy', that Dusty added to his repertoire.

Fed up with waiting, my mother took me to the station, and on passing the pub, we could hear Dusty giving his rendition of the song.

Leaving me outside, she went into the pub and said, "Come on, you're taking my sonny boy to Hastings." He left without an argument.

One Christmas, coming home from the pub, he saw a tramp, and he insisted that he come home with him for dinner. Gran said that the tramp felt uncomfortable sharing dinner with us and he asked if she could pack some food for him. She did so and he went on his way.

I remember Christmases as joyful occasions. Mum would buy little bundles of coloured strips of paper, and we would glue them together, to make paper chains. She would then fix them to the ceiling with drawing pins. We could not afford a tree, so I would hang up a pillowcase for my presents.

Even after they moved to Cranbrook, Gran and Dusty would 'come home' to us for the holiday. There always seemed to be food that we never had ordinarily. There would be pheasants and rabbits hanging in the scullery, and Dusty would bring home a small barrel of beer called a pin. This held forty-three pints of beer, and he would fix it up on top of the copper.

We always had a leg of pork and sometimes a goose. There was a bowl of fruit on the sideboard, and the fire was lit in the front room.

Gran made the Christmas pudding, and when this was dished up, one slice always had a sixpence in it. She always made sure that I was given this slice, much to my delight.

We would usually go to a pub in Priory Road called 'The Bell', and there would be singing and much laughter. Gran rarely drank, but at Christmas, after she had a couple of port and lemons, even she could be persuaded to sing. Dusty had a 'squeeze box' (an accordion) that he played, and he also played the spoons. He would perform conjuring tricks that got him some free pints.

Because of the law, I wasn't allowed in the bar where drinks were served, but at Christmas I would be smuggled in. Sometimes, the others in the bar would give me as much as half a crown to do an impersonation of George Formby. I would imitate the ukulele by making a noise at the back of my throat. Back at home we would play darts and other games like Ludo and Snakes and Ladders.

One game that we made up, was for someone to sit on a stool in the doorway, facing into the front room. A tin of fruit was placed on top of the person's head. Then the others would all stand out in the scullery and throw ping pong balls to try and knock it off. The tin was too heavy to shift, so dad took a cabbage and hurled it. It struck mum, who was sitting there, on the back of the neck, knocking her off the stool and the tin went flying. This caused great hilarity.

In summer, Gran and Dusty would hire a beach chalet at Winchelsea. They took me with them, and mum and dad would join us at weekends. We would fish for shrimps, using nets with a flat wooden bottom, that was pushed along the sand at low tide. Dusty had a large tin-can that he fixed to his belt and we would fill it with shrimps. When we got back, Gran would cook them for tea.

One weekend we all went to Pett Level, when the tide was out, to collect winkles from the exposed rocks. Dusty and dad rolled up their trousers and Mum and Gran tucked their dresses into their knickers, and we paddled our way out through the rocks.

21

When we were a long way out to sea, we failed to notice the tide coming in quickly behind us. Soon we were cut off from the shore with the tide rapidly rising around us. Trying to get back, we stumbled over the submerged rocks, cutting our feet. Dad put me on his shoulders, and we struggled back with Mum beside us.

Gran and Dusty were further out, and as I looked back, I could see her half submerged with her dress floating around her. She couldn't swim and had given up. Dusty went back and grabbed her, he then half dragged half swam with her back to safety.

I kept saying, "Mummy, where are the lifeboat men?"

A beach attendant took us to a first-aid hut to sponge and bandage our feet. However, we had managed to save some of the winkles and when we got back to the chalet Gran cooked them. As the saucepan came to the boil, I remember hearing them whistle.

Nearby there was a clubhouse called the 39 Club. I think it cost two shillings to join and we would go there on Saturday nights. Downstairs had a bar, and upstairs was a dance hall with a band and tables and chairs. Dad and Dusty would stay in the bar playing darts, and Mum, Gran and I would go up to the dance hall. We would have drinks and sandwiches and watch the dancers. Sometimes Mum or Gran would waltz me round the floor. There was a balcony, and I can still picture the moonlight reflecting on the calm sea.

My paternal grandparents lived in a row of old cottages behind Woolworths in Tunbridge Wells. My father worked as a porter at the Calverley Hotel. Even after he married, he still had to go to his father's house to take the evening papers to his father, before coming home to my mother and me in Tonbridge.

I only have scant recollection of my paternal grandparents. Grandfather Mat was a gruff, thickset old man with a ruddy face. My grandmother Alice was his second wife. My father was an only son, but there was a half-sister by the previous marriage. They never kept in touch. Grandmother Alice worked as a cleaner at the Catholic church and my father was brought up as a Catholic, although he followed no religion.

A woman resident at the hotel where my father worked had a brother who was the vicar at St. Mary's High Church in Hadlow. On her insistence I was christened there. Other than that, I was never taken to church as neither my mother nor my father were religious.

I remember that one day I was taken to Sunday school by some older boys in our road. I wanted to sit with them at the front but I was constantly removed to the back of the hall to play in the sand tray with the other toddlers. This didn't please me, and I so would never go again.

Sometimes, as a child, my father would take me on a Sunday morning to see his parents. Grandfather Mat would be sitting on a wooden chair on the pavement outside his cottage, which had a low, dark entrance. He would sit there smoking a large meerschaum pipe, waiting for the pub at the end of the road to open. He was a heavy drinker and he would always go to the pub at lunchtimes. He used to just nod his head at me and grunt, and that's the only contact that I had with them.

Gran and Dusty, my mother's parents, were completely different. Like my mother, they idolized me, especially my grandfather Henry George Rhodes, known to everyone as 'Dusty'. He was a great character and he played an important part in my life, as did my grandmother Clara.

Dusty was a post office wireman at this time. Born in 1880, as a boy he had gone to the ragged school. His father was a painter and a sign writer who mixed his own paints. Lead was used extensively in paints, and he died of painter's colic (lead poisoning) when Dusty was young. I think that his mother couldn't cope, and at fifteen, Dusty was sent to the 'Arethusa' and the 'Chichester' Training Ships.

He served four years, he was awarded three Good Conduct Badges and when he left in 1899, he was awarded the Arethusa Prize Knife for Good Conduct.

His certificate 'For Boys of Good Character' makes interesting reading:

'This is to Certify that Henry George Rhodes (No. 57) knows how to reef and is able to furl small sails. He can heave the lead and give the soundings; make all bends, knots and splices; knows the flags according to the Commercial Code; can swim; pull in a boat; keep his clothes in repair; read, write, and do common arithmetic'.

I believe that this training stood him in good stead for the rest of his life. He worked as the Town Lamplighter and then as a drayman for R.

Whites, who made and bottled lemonade in Tonbridge. He met my grandmother, who worked there, and they married in 1905.

My Gran never spoke of her upbringing, although she once told me that as a girl, she was so hungry at times, that she scavenged food from dustbins. Her mother was in service, so this was probably for the kitchen scraps. When she reached the age of sixty, she applied for her state pension and was asked to supply her birth certificate. She had to apply to Somerset House to obtain a copy and she was very upset to find that she was illegitimate. She was told that she did not qualify, as she had not made sufficient contributions, so she got a job as a school cleaner for several years, in order to qualify for her pension.

She always vowed never to be poor again and she was very thrifty. This did not make her mean, as she had a generous nature. She held the purse strings in their marriage and 'Dusty' was content to let her manage their money.

She used to instil into me that: "a man's best friend is his bank book," and "honesty is the best policy." She put money into the Post Office savings book that she started for me and she encouraged me to do the same. It paid two and a half percent interest per annum. Sixpenny savings stamps could be bought at the Post Office and stuck into a booklet. When this was full of forty stamps, the pound it represented would be transferred into your bank book.

There was also a rectangular metal box, about the size of two cigarette packets, shaped like a small book. This was covered with red leather and it had an entry slot in one end, where coins could be inserted. This end had steel pins that opened inwards to allow coins to go in but swivelled shut to prevent any coins from being taken out. It had a lock on one side and was hinged on the other. My mother held the key and when it was full, she would take it to the Post Office and deposit the money into my savings book.

When I needed some money, I found that by inserting the blades of two kitchen knives through the pins, far enough to keep them apart, I could twist and shake the box until I got a coin between the blades, and then it would slide out. Sometimes Mum and Gran wondered why the money box was taking so long to fill up, in spite of all the coins that were being put into it.

Both my Grandfathers had known each other prior to my birth. During the First World War they had shared lodgings in Dover. They had been sent there to work on the communications between the shore batteries guarding the coast. Dusty would tell the story of how, when the German Zeppelins came over at night, Mat Saunders, who was the foreman, would lock himself inside their bedroom and he would leave Dusty to sit on the landing to comfort the landlady. When the German Zeppelins were overhead, the anti-aircraft guns would open up, and she would quiver and shake, and it was left to Dusty to console her and to calm her down.

When they were working laying the wires for the guns, Grandfather Mat would leave Dusty in charge of the others and go off to the pub. Mat would think nothing of consuming eight pints at lunchtime and then come back and sleep it off.

On Saturday nights, all the men would go out drinking till closing time. Full of beer they then returned to their lodgings. Sometimes as many as five had to share a room. There was no toilet upstairs, and the only way of relieving themselves was to use an enamel chamber pot. When this reached thumb high, they would empty it out of the bedroom window.

One night Dusty dropped it and it hit the cobbles and rattled off down the path. In the morning, he had to explain this to the landlady and apologize. She said that she had wondered what had been killing her chrysanthemums.

Chapter 3

My mother had not been trained as a needlewoman, but taught herself, and she made all my clothes and many of her own. It was the time of the Great Depression of the nineteen thirties. She had a Jones Sewing Machine and she would sit at the kitchen table for hours, making clothes. Her patterns came from magazines, or from old clothes that she stripped apart and copied. Sometimes, she could earn money by making clothes for some of the neighbours, who would come to our house for fittings.

When I was about three, she made me a velvet suit and a frilly blouse with fancy cuffs. She took me to a studio in the town to be photographed. I'm standing by a table with a goldfish bowl on it, dressed in the suit, with matching velvet shoes. The photographer took an impromptu shot of me holding the bowl with one hand, with the fingers of my other hand in the water, chasing the fish. I still have the hand-coloured photo and I look like a very angelic Little Lord Fauntleroy.

Dusty's job as a wireman was moved to a depot in Cranbrook and he used to cycle the seventeen miles each way every morning and every night. On Friday nights when he'd collected his pay, he would put part of it in his inside pocket to pay my Gran, and the rest he would use to call into the pubs along the way home.

One night after dark when he hadn't arrived home, Gran went off to find him. After walking several miles, she came to the Carpenters Arms, a pub in Tudeley. Dusty was there and she could hear him singing.

Gran was a little woman, normally rather meek but nevertheless determined. Back then women would seldom enter a pub alone, but after waiting outside for some time, she plucked up courage and entered the small bar that was used for takeaway sales.

Dusty was in the Public Bar entertaining the occupants. When the barman came through to her, she asked him to tell Harry Rhodes that his wife was there.

When the barman told Dusty, he said, "You must be mistaken, my wife would never come here, you must mean Harry Rose."

Gran then looked around the partition and she told him that she had come to take him home.

When they got outside, he collected his bike and said, "Get on the crossbar mother, I'll ride you home." She refused, and she told him that he was drunk. He said, "All right, then you can walk home."

With that, he mounted the bicycle and rode off leaving her. He hadn't gone far when he fell off. Gran picked him up, and half walked, half dragged him along the road, until she became exhausted. She then left him lying by the side of the road while she went back for his bicycle. She continued to do this until, about halfway home, when she came to a bridge over a small stream.

She left Dusty hanging over it while she went back again for the bike. As she came back with it, Dusty climbed onto the bridge and called back to her that he'd been a bugger to her all his life, and she'd be better off without him. With that he jumped off the bridge to the stream below.

Gran dropped the bike and ran towards him, but when she looked over the bridge the stream was dried up. She dragged him out and she managed to get him as far as the bottom of our road, where she left him lying beside a pond on the lawn of Vale House, a large property there.

Going home she found that her half-brother, Sid, was there with my mother, who was teaching him to read and write. Sid was a tall man who worked as a stoker at the gasworks. She told him what had happened with Dusty and she asked if he would go and get him.

When Sid found Dusty and shone the torch on him, Dusty looked up and said, "All right officer, I'll come quietly."

***

Dusty pestered my Gran until she agreed that he could buy a motorbike to travel from Tonbridge to Cranbrook, instead of having to cycle each way to the depot. He went into Tunbridge Wells and bought it and the man showed him how to start it. There was no licence or test required then, nor I think, was insurance needed. Having been shown how, Dusty kick-started the motor bike and rode it back to Tonbridge.

Gran, my mother and I were outside our house as he came down the road, and as we waved, he just rode past. He continued to circle down and around the railway bridge and then back again past us. Everyone thought that he was just showing off but in fact he did not know how to stop it. He finally stopped it by shouting for us to watch out and he ran it into our front door.

As he got more proficient, he would go up to the pub on Sunday lunchtimes, and at turn out time he would ride home and pick me up and sit me on the tank in front of him, for a circular trip around the road. My mother would jump on the pillion behind him, saying that if he was going to kill her child, she'd die too.

These machines had a pump that had to be pumped at regular intervals to provide the lubricant to the engine. Dusty would forget this and the engine would suddenly seize up, bringing the bike to an abrupt stop. He would have to wait until it cooled down for the oil to be pumped to the engine and then restart it.

For driving at night there was a detachable lamp in front that had to be filled with crystals. Then water was added to produce a gas which was then ignited to provide a light. Coming home from work on a Friday night and calling into the pubs along the way, the lamp would run out of water and the light would go out. Always resourceful, Dusty would urinate into it and this would soon act on the crystals to provide him with enough light to see his way home.

When I was about three, Gran and Dusty moved to Cranbrook to be near to the depot where his job was. They rented Crown Cottage, an old white wooden fronted cottage in the High Street, with a white picket fence in front. Next door, over the passage archway, was an adjoining cottage that joined onto The Crown Hotel. At the time of writing, and with the aid of Google maps, I am amazed to see that it's still there today, exactly as it was then, including the white picket fence.

My mother made me a jacket with two open pleats at the back. Every few days in summer the ice cream man would come down our road. He rode a tricycle with a large wooden icebox between the front wheels. As soon as I heard his bell, I would run in for a "guidey-gah", and then off for an ice cream. My father told me that I used to run everywhere, and when I ran around the corner, all they saw were the pleats of the jacket disappearing. They called it my flying jacket.

Fathers job was a porter at the Calverley Hotel in Tunbridge Wells, and he would come home late at night. He used to bring food from their kitchens home with him, and I was brought downstairs from the bedroom so that I could enjoy a late supper. I can still remember the taste of that chicken broth and sandwiches, and nothing I've eaten since has tasted better. Chicken in those days was a luxury in our house.

Another time, when I was seven years old, I was allowed to get up in the early hours, to listen to the radio commentary from the Yankee Stadium New York.

The British Heavyweight Boxing Champion was a Welshman named Tommy Farr, and he was fighting Joe Louis for the world title. We thought that Tommy had won, but he lost on a controversial points decision after fifteen rounds.

***

My father was out of work when the hotel suddenly closed down. He was put on the 'Dole' which was twenty-nine shillings (£1.45) a week, from which my mother paid seven shillings a week rent. Then she had to feed us and keep house on the rest. I can remember some weeks sitting on the stairs with my mother and being told to keep quiet, when the rent man called.

She paid a few pence a week house insurance. Sometimes she would get old towels and tea cloths that had holes in them and scorch them around the edges by holding them over the gas ring. Then when the insurance man called, she would say they had caught fire and we would get a few shillings compensation.

A Mrs Richardson from down the road was an agent for a club that issued vouchers for sums up to thirty shillings. Mum would get these and pay back sixpence or a shilling a week. This meant that she could use the vouchers to buy essentials like household goods.

In the spring, mum would get a job 'hop tying'. There were lots of fields growing hops all over Kent and the young sprouting hop vines would be trained around strings that were attached to rows of wires, supported on tall poles. Kent was called 'the Garden of England' with many apple and cherry orchards. It was also where many hops were grown.

Tonbridge, and neighbouring Paddock Wood, were the hub of acres of hop fields. These were ready to be harvested in August and September and a small army of casual pickers was required. Many hundreds of Londoners from the East End would descend on the town, coming down by train and then making their way to the various farms that employed them. It was mostly women and children, and their menfolk would come at weekends and also during their holidays. They would stay in 'hopping huts' in Paddock Wood. Whitbread had their farms and large oast houses there, with the kilns for the hop drying.

There were two farms near us that had hop fields, and mum would book early to work there, to ensure that she could earn some extra cash.

During the late summer we would go hop picking. Mum had an old pram that she would load up with a stool and bottles of powdered lemonade, and make sausage rolls and sandwiches, packed up in an old biscuit tin. Wet weather clothing and wellingtons were also included, together with a large umbrella. She would push the pram, with me toddling beside her, hanging onto the handle, down our road to the hop fields.

We would have to go through the sewerage works, where there were three large open tanks filled with effluent, that were constantly being stirred by large metal paddles. From time to time, these tanks would be emptied and spread onto the surrounding fields that had cabbages grown on them. These would grow to huge sizes and when they were cooked the smell was horrible.

I can remember her struggling to push the pram through the mud on wet days, with me holding onto the handles. But mostly I remember the swirling mist and the early morning dew of autumn, with the sun breaking through to produce warm sunny days.

On arrival at the field, everyone jostled for the end of the row that looked to have the best bunches of hops. A horse drawn dray would bring a load of 'bins' and these would be strung out along the rows, ready for the start of picking.

Each bin was made of sacking, with two long poles with cross pieces each end, that swivelled to open. The hessian was nailed to the poles to form a large purse. This was the 'bin'. Some had a sacking piece inserted in the middle to provide a 'half bin' for single pickers. At nine o'clock a whistle was blown, and everyone began picking.

The bins would fit between the rows of hop vines, that had twined themselves around strings. They ran up from the ground to a system of wires, about ten feet high. These were called 'bines', and were pulled down so that the hops could be picked and put into the bin Then you would move the bin up the row for the next lot.

On arriving at the hop field on the first day, you were given a tally book. There would be lots of pickers and everyone would try to get the best position.

Sometimes when the bines were pulled down, the string would break, leaving the 'head' up on the wires. These were the best hops and you would call for the 'pole-puller'. He would come with a long wooden pole that had a sharp hook at the top and cut them down.

When the 'measurer' came around, he would empty each bin, using a bushel basket, calling out the count as he did. The tally lady would record the number of bushels and mark it in the picker's book.

Another man would hold a large sack called a 'poke', into which the hops were tipped. When it was full, the end was secured, and it was loaded onto a horse drawn trailer and taken to the oast house. The adults would sit on the edge of the bin and pick, and the children would sit on stools or upturned baskets and pick into anything that could hold the hops. When they had picked enough, these were tipped into the bin. I used to pick into an upturned umbrella.

Some measurers would gently 'fluff' the hops into the bushel basket, while others would ram them in which meant that they totalled less for your book. The hops had also to be 'clean', with no leaves. Some measurers were more particular about this than others.

At twelve thirty p.m. a whistle would blow, and picking would stop for lunch. I'll never forget the taste of the sandwiches and the lemonade. The whistle was blown again at one p.m. and picking would start again and go on until four thirty p.m., when the call came to pull no more bines.

When the rows were finished, the trailer would take your bin to the next field and you would start again. It was important to get to the end of your row as quickly as possible, so that you got the choice of the best hops in the next field.

By the end of each day's picking, your fingers were black with a thick gunge that was difficult to remove. That came from the hop pollen. I loved the smell of the hops and I remember it well. Unless you had a 'sub' part way through, all the money that you earned was paid out at the end of the hopping season. The rate you received varied from year to year and from farm to farm. I think it was usually between sixpence and a shilling a bushel (2½p and 5p).

At the end of hopping, on the last day, the women (especially the Londoners) would chase the measurers, they would throw anyone who they caught into a bin full of hops, and wrestle to pull off his trousers. There was no such thing as sexual harassment in those days. There was much laughter and banter, as can be imagined.

The East Enders who lived in the 'hopper huts', would decorate them and even put wallpaper on the walls. They would light campfires with cooking pots and sing and dance in the evenings. It was their annual holiday, especially at weekends when the menfolk would come down. There would be some drunkenness in the pubs but not much violence that I remember.

Chapter 4

My father had never done physical work, but in those days if a job became available you had to take it or lose your dole money. The Southern Railway was the town's biggest employer, and to his credit, my father, who had never been accustomed to manual work, got a job as a labourer.

They had gangs of men called 'platelayers' who repaired and renewed the tracks. It was hard physical work and he would come home exhausted from shovelling stone and his hands would be blistered. There were no gloves or protective clothing then, nor mechanical diggers to do the hard work.

He also suffered a lot with his stomach and indigestion. He always pulled his armchair up to the table to eat his meal, and I remember many times seeing him push his plate away, with the food uneaten.

The perspiration would trickle down his forehead. For years he would suck Rennies by the boxful. He never saw a doctor. There was no NHS then, only some charitable schemes, although some doctors would give their services free. My father was fiercely independent, and he would never accept charity. A doctor's visit to the house cost two shillings and sixpence (12½p).

In a letter from Gran to me at the time, she wrote, "I hope your dad is feeling better, I am sending him a box of tablets to take. They do Grandad a lot of good when he has pains in his tummy, so tell him to try them."

Both my parents were heavy smokers. Mum smoked Craven A and dad Players full strength Capstan Navy Cut. In each packet there were cigarette cards and you could collect them and put them into albums. When my albums were full, I would take the 'twicers' to school and swap them.

Dad smoked all his life, but when he reached eighty, he gave up. When I asked him why he had given up after all this time, he said that he didn't want to get lung cancer.

He died aged ninety-two and on the death certificate it said that he had suffered from Chronic Obstructive Pulmonary Disease (C.O.P.D.) for twenty years.

He was a lifelong socialist and in later years he despised me for my political beliefs, calling me a bloody Tory. Strangely, he admired the Duke of Windsor and he thought he should have been allowed to marry Mrs Simpson and become the King. The Duke had visited the coal mines during the depression and he had said that something should be done to help the miners. Nothing came of it, but my father always held him in high esteem after that.

During this period, we had an allotment along the railway embankment that my father was entitled to, but he was no gardener and my mother did most of it, including the digging. My job was to collect buckets of water from a stream to keep the plants growing. Looking back, it seems we enjoyed much drier and longer summers then.

We also kept chickens and one day whilst feeding them the usual scraps, my mother noticed that one hen was looking poorly. On picking it up she found that its crop bag was swollen, with what could be seen as a large lump inside it. The hen was in a sorry state and close to death, so Mum decided to operate.

She had no veterinary training, but she was a resourceful woman. She told me to hold it by clamping my hands over its wings, while she took a razor blade and slit the crop bag open. There was a horrible smell as a large slimy ball of fermenting long grass came out. Mum then washed it out with an antiseptic, she then took a needle and thread and she sewed it up. I'm happy to say that the hen fully recovered, and she continued to lay eggs.

Across the small yard from our backdoor, was next doors back door. Each house had a brick path that led down past the lavatories, and then ran along the back of all the houses in the row. From there, each house had a strip of garden running down to the river.

This was a tributary of the river Medway. On the wall between our house and next door, we had a nail on which our galvanized bath hung.

Next door they would catch large dragonflies and stick them on the wall, using hat pins. This family was named Pankhurst and there were three sons, all older than me. Mrs Pankhurst was a big woman always dressed in a wraparound apron, and her husband was a little man with 'consumption' (TB) and he was always coughing and spitting.

I would rarely enter their house, but when I did, I remember that their kitchen table was always covered with knives, forks and all manner of crockery. He would be sitting beside the fireplace, and there was an old horsehair sofa under the window that was piled high with newspapers. Behind the back door was a pyramid of tea leaves where they used to empty the tea pot onto the brick floor. When they could not open the door, one of the sons would remove them and spread them on the garden.

They had a tabby cat which always seemed to be having kittens. When they could not find anyone who wanted one, they would get rid of them by drowning them in a bucket of water. They eventually decided to get rid of the cat, and I watched their sons as they struggled to put it into a large sack. Then, as one held it, the other one put some bricks in and tied the top.

I followed them down the garden and watched as they hurled it into the river. It sank at first but then came up to the surface as the cat fought furiously to free itself. It finally managed to get out and swam away. It never came back.

An investigation found that they had lice next door. They had penetrated through the wall into our side and they were feeding on the wallpaper paste. My mother used to make it by mixing powder and flour and water. This meant both houses had to be fumigated and we had to move out for several days while the work was carried out.

***

We had a cat called Ginger and a spaniel puppy named Chum. I loved playing with him in the garden or in the house, where I would dress him up in my old clothes. His life was short as he caught distemper. We treated him with Bob Martin powders as we could not afford a vet, but he died.

Our garden ran down to the river and in winter it would often flood and come up to our back door. There was a shed at the bottom and mum had built a chicken run there. Next to that were the rabbit hutches made from old wooden boxes. We could not afford proper hinges, so the doors were hung with strips of old leather that were nailed on, and the door was secured with a wooden peg. I also kept guinea pigs there.

We also had two homing pigeons. One day when mum hadn't anything to feed us for dinner, she decided that they would have to go. She had managed to catch one by its feet and she held it as it flapped its wings, calling my father to clasp his hands over it. He was never any good at this sort of thing and just grabbed its tail feathers. The pigeon then flew off, leaving its feathers in his hands. I do not remember if it came back or what happened to the other one.

Along our row of terraced houses were families with similar backgrounds to us, although most were better off. The other side of the alleyway, towards the town, there was a row of five. The first one was rented by a widow and a son named Norman about my age. Her surname was Hatterway and his was Ward. I do not know their history, but I remember that she was crippled with arthritis. Some of the other boys and I would torment them.

Further up the road there was a break in the railway embankment wall, where the road went under a bridge. We would go to the end where there were some foot holes and climb over and go back along the other side. Then we would throw a string down to another boy, who would drape it over the lamppost outside her house and tie it to her front door knocker. When it was nearly dark, we would rattle her knocker till she opened the door to see who it was. It took some time before she realised what we were up to.

Sometimes we would all play cricket in the road. A wicket would be chalked on the railway wall and the bowler would run up the passage to the pavement and then bowl the ball across the road. The game was frequently interrupted by the Tarmac lorries that went up and down.

One day when batting, I slogged the ball and it went straight through someone's window, further along the road. We all scattered but they found out who did it and mum had to get it repaired. After that we could only play if we went to the Botany field, although we were not really allowed there.

At the top of the road was the station goods yard. Parcels that came by train were delivered by a horse drawn wagon, the driver of which was Bob Starnes. Bob lived a few doors up. He had lost one leg in an accident and he had a wooden stump.

Sometimes he would put a nosebag on the horse and leave it outside his house, while he went in for a cup of tea. When he came out, as soon as he removed the nosebag, the old horse would trot off. I would laugh to see him with his wooden leg, trying to scramble up into the driving seat.

***

There was a little shop at the corner of The Botany and opposite to that was a small factory making Latter's ice cream. Further down the road was a little shop run by Elsie Laurence. It was only the front room of her house, and when you went in, the doorbell would ring, and she would come through from the back. Mum would send me down for her cigarettes and odds and ends. These were put 'on the book' and settled once a week.

Her husband worked at the Baltic Sawmills in the town and he had lost his right hand in an accident. He had a metal plate on the end of his wrist and a hook. He rode a motor bike by removing the hook and fitting the plate to an attachment on the handlebars. This was enclosed in a gauntlet glove. I would watch him in awe as he rode past dressed in his cap and goggles and wearing a long leather overcoat.

Every Saturday night there was a collection of market traders with stalls, at the entrance to the railway goods yard. When they were packing, up my parents would take me there so that mum could see what they hadn't sold and barter with them to buy cheap meat and vegetables, and any fruit that they had left over.

I can remember eating overripe bananas. With the meat, Mum would make a meat pudding in a basin with a cloth tied over it. This would be boiled on the gas stove or the kitchen range. When it was sliced up there was lots of pudding, with some little pieces of meat in the middle. Any pieces of pudding that were left over we would have with some syrup on it for 'afters'.

Tonbridge was a market town with a cattle market at the top end of the High Street. There were some one hundred and thirty shops. On market days, cattle would often be herded down the High Street to the railway goods yard, where they would be loaded into cattle trucks. Sometimes some of them would escape and run into the shops, causing chaos.

***

Once a year, the circus would come to town. Many of the animals came by rail and they were unloaded in the goods yard. They would then be taken along the High Street, the elephants walking and the lions and the tigers in cages on trailers, pulled by steam engines. The 'big top' was erected on the Botany field where it stayed for a week.

There were three 'picture houses' one was the Star cinema, it was close to the river and the rats used to run around the floor. When the river flooded, your feet would get wet if you were sitting down in the front. There was also a roller-skating rink, which was a large wooden building where auctions were sometimes held. I can remember being taken there to see magic lantern shows.

I also remember the Home and Colonial shop that sold foodstuffs. There was a good-looking woman who wore a white apron, with her dark hair tied into a neat bun at the back. She would cut butter from a large lump and using wooden 'bats' she would knock it into small 'pats' and put them on the counter for sale. There was a black and white tiled floor, with sawdust spread on it where the meat was sold. The carcasses would be taken down from hooks behind the counter and cut up into joints. Butcher shops also had sawdust on their floors, to soak up the blood.

There was another shop called 'Gunners' that sold haberdashery. Mum would take me there when she bought material. I was always fascinated by what happened at the counter when a purchase was paid for. The assistant would reach up and take down a metal cup that was screwed into a base and was attached to a system of overhead wires. These ran around under the shop ceiling.

The money was placed in the cup and screwed into the base. Then the assistant would reach up and pull the handle that hung underneath. The cup whizzed off under the ceiling around the room, changing direction through many junctions, to finish up at a small kiosk.

The lady cashier would then unscrew it, take out the money, write out a ticket and then replace it with any change. Then she would pull the handle and off it would whizz again, back to the counter. I loved going there just to watch this display.

I always enjoyed playing in the garden and along the riverbank. I would make tunnels in the dirt, create miniature roads and play with my dinky toy cars. Overlooking the river, we had an old elderberry tree and I made a camp there, using old coconut matting. Sometimes I took lemonade and some food and had a picnic. I fished using worms for bait, and the gudgeon that I caught my mother would cook.

Toys were only given at Christmas and on birthdays, but I remember always receiving plenty of items. There were picture books, games like Ludo and Snakes and Ladders, humming tops, dinky cars, lead soldiers, forts, Hornby train sets and Meccano, which was strips of metal that bolted together.

I particularly liked making things with the Meccano set and there was a shop on the station arch in town, called 'Cyco Radio', that sold electrical appliances. It also had other odds and ends, including a box of all sorts of Meccano pieces.

Mum would give me sixpence a week pocket money when she could afford it, for helping her in the house. I remember one day going to the shop with a shilling to buy several odd pieces. I was building a model crane and there was still one piece that I needed, but I had used up my money.

When the man turned away to serve another customer, I took it and I slipped it into my pocket. After that, whenever I played with my Meccano, I could never bring myself to use this piece as I felt so guilty at having taken it. It was only worth a penny or two but my Gran's saying that 'honesty was always the best policy' always reminded me that I'd stolen it.

Mum bought me a large second-hand rocking horse from someone who had outgrown it. I would sit astride it and imagine that I was a real cowboy, dressed in some old chaps and with a pistol and holster. I had a replica six shooter that could be loaded with 'caps'. These were rolls of narrow paper with the 'caps' spaced along them. When loaded into the gun these would revolve and when the trigger was pulled it resulted in a loud bang. I would aim at our cat or dog and the bang would cause them to quickly disappear.

***

One birthday, Gran and Dusty sent Mum the money to buy me my first bicycle. It was second-hand and when we went to collect it, Mum was surprised to see me get on and ride off straight away. I soon learned to run alongside and leap into the saddle like the cowboys did on their horses. This was rather tricky, as if you timed it wrong, you sat down on your testicles which was eye-watering.

***

The Ritz Cinema opened in the 'Botany' in 1937 and every Saturday morning children could go. There was a club called the 'Good Old Union Chums' and at the start of each performance we would sing songs that had the words projected onto the screen. I think the entrance fee cost threepence, but I remember that you could also take bottles and jam jars and be let in for nothing.

Most of the films were about "Cowboys and Indians". Some had been real cowboys, like Tom Mix, Buck Jones and Hopalong Cassidy. The good guy always wore a white Stetson and rode a white (grey) horse. The bad guys wore black and always got their comeuppance.

I used to play Cowboys and Indians with the other boys, and I remember hiding behind our shed and waiting for one of the others to peep from around the passage. I had an old air rifle and I would shoot at them, aiming above their heads so that the pellet hit the brickwork. I could not understand why it didn't ricochet like it did in the Westerns.

I also had a Webley Air Pistol. The barrel was fitted with a lever at one end, allowing it to be pulled up to set the spring. This exposed the breach. When I could not get lead pellets, I found that by pushing the gun barrel into a potato that it would leave a plug, so that when the gun was fired it became the bullet. This had a limited range so I could only use it at close quarters.

I also practised throwing my sheath knife at the shed door but I could never get it to stick like the Indians did. I also threw our small axe like a tomahawk, but without success. I had better luck with a bow and arrow that I made. I would take a piece of willow and bend it and tie it with a piece of string. For the arrow I used a stick and cut a slit at one end and fitted a paper flight. At the other end I fitted a two-inch nail. At first it wouldn't fly properly as it wasn't heavy enough, so I took some old lead soldiers and I melted them down on our gas stove. Then I made a mould and I poured the molten lead around the nail. This worked well until the nail fell out of the arrow.

***

Further down the road, on the end house by another passageway, was a family called Cosham. Tom Cosham was an engine driver and there was a son called Les and a daughter called Hilda. Like most of the other children in our road, they were older than me. Mrs Cosham was rarely seen out of the house. Mr Cosham had a shed at the bottom of the garden, made of old railway sleepers. He had a workshop inside, and he used to make model railway engines. It was next to the river and they had built a wooden landing stage and strung a wire across the river to a post on the other side.

They had made a raft of old empty oil drums that could then be used as a ferry, to cross the river to the other side. When the river was low, and they were at work, I could go along under the bank from our garden, and then use it to cross over to the field and to the woods over by the gas works.

I would play there in the trees, pretending that I was Tarzan. An Olympic swimmer named Johnny Weissmuller played Tarzan in a series of films, and he would swing on vines from tree to tree in the jungle. He had a loud wailing call that I could imitate.

I had a collection of old ropes that I strung up in the trees, so that I could do it. I remember one time a rope broke, and I fell from quite a height, landing flat on my back. I wasn't hurt, but it winded me and I was gasping for breath for several minutes. I never told my mother as she never knew that I went there.

Across the passageway from the Cosham's was the Swan family. Old man Frank Swan and his wife Maud had three sons. Ron, Norman and Derek. Derek was the youngest and he was a couple of years older than me.

When the Cosham's bought a flat bottom canoe, Les would take Derek and me with him and we would paddle down river until we reached the 'dump'. That was where the council dumped all the town waste. It was a huge pile of rotting rubbish close to the river. It was alive with rats and we would take our air rifles and shoot them. My air rifle was a Diana and the most accurate of any that I owned.

In 1935 there was a National Rat Catching Week, and the Tonbridge rat-catchers chalked up four hundred and sixty-seven kills, making Tonbridge the national champions. Despite this, there were still plenty left over for us to shoot.

Further along the road, Harry Newman had a shed in his garden where he did shoe repairs. He was by trade a 'snob' (cobbler). He had all the machines for shoemaking, and he would cut and stitch the leather soles and heels onto boots and shoes. This was expensive to have done.

Mum bought stick-on rubber soles and heels to repair ours, and metal heel tips that she would nail on. Harry kept a .410 shotgun and if anyone spotted a river rat on the bank opposite, they would run to him and he would grab his gun and try to shoot it.

Another boy called Ivor Neal, who was my age, would often play with Derek and me. The Neal's lived two doors away from us. Charlie Neal was a driver for the Tarmac company at the bottom of the road, and a part-time fireman. His wife Grace was a kindly woman who would sometimes help my mother out when times were hard.

Us boys would sometimes make our way to the Botany river bridge and play underneath it where there was a dam and a waterfall. Under the bridge, two large metal sewerage pipes spanned the river and we would cross on them and throw anything that would float into the river and watch it go over the dam.

One day scrambling along the bank I slipped, and I fell in. I couldn't swim then, as my mother had not allowed me to go to the school's swimming lessons. She was afraid that I might catch something from the other boys. I remember going under and swallowing a lot of water and being unable to breathe. Luckily, when I surfaced, Derek was on the bank near enough to pull me out. Ivor ran home to my mother, telling her that I'd fallen in the river.

She said, "Is he drowned?"

Ivor said, "Yes".

She rushed up towards the bridge to be met by me squelching my way home.

Derek and I became good friends and I can remember us both sitting on top of the railway embankment wall, with our legs dangling over the edge. We were watching the tarmac (South-Eastern Tar Distillers SETAR) lorries going by, and the pedestrians on the pavement on the other side.

A woman went by pushing a pram, and I asked Derek where babies came from. He said that they came out of the woman's belly. I then asked him how they got there. He said that the man puts them there.

"How do they do that?" I asked.

He replied, "The man pokes his winkle in."

I said, "What does he do then, just piddle?" Derek said that he didn't know.

***

Derek and I, with a boy called Lionel Weddell, who lived further up the road, would make trolley carts from scrap wooden crates and old pram wheels. These carts had the larger pram wheels at the back of the crate, and a cross piece where you sat. At the front was an extended timber shaft that had a cross piece to which the two smaller pram wheels were fitted. This cross piece was bolted to the shaft so that it swivelled, and a rope was attached to each side and used to guide the cart. In order to stop you had to put your foot on each front wheel.

At the bottom of Vale Road there was the Tarmac works on one side and the sewage works and stables on the other. Vale House came next, where the road bent and went up a steep hill to the railway bridge. We would pull our carts to the top of the hill, then sit in them and hurtle off downhill.

The challenge was to see who could get the farthest along the road past the Tarmac works, before you ran out of propulsion. It was a test of courage to see how fast you went, in order to gather enough speed to go the furthest. If you were unlucky enough to meet a tar lorry coming up, or the horses from the sewage works, it took a quick reaction to try to avoid them. If you tried to turn too sharply, the cart would tip over, spilling you onto the tarmac. I suffered quite a few bruises and grazes from the tarmac, before I became adept at this manoeuvre. Explaining these to my mother wasn't easy, as she had forbidden me to do it.

Coming home from school I would play marbles along the gutter with the other boys. Everyone you hit became yours. I was good at it and I had several boxes full.

I cut prongs from tree branches to make catapults. You could buy the rubber elastic, and I made leather thongs. This resulted in a powerful weapon and the marbles made effective missiles. I'd line up jam jars and tin cans along the fence and aim at them. Sometimes the target would be a neighbour's cat.

There were times when Ivor and I would fight, and he would go home to his mother, crying. She would then come around to our house and give me sixpence to make up and to be friends again. This was good as I could then use it to go to the pictures.

As we got older, we were allowed to catch the train to London to do some shopping and look around the West End. Not far from Charring Cross Station was the Windmill Theatre. This theatre put-on variety shows, and many famous comedians began their careers there. Even during the Blitz, the theatre stayed open and their famous slogan was 'We Never Closed'.

Their speciality was the nude tableaus. The dancing girls covered their vital parts with fans, and when they were standing still the fans were removed to reveal all.

Until the 1960s Britain had very strict laws on alcohol, gambling and all forms of nudity. This show evaded the law on displaying nudity. Anyone under sixteen wasn't allowed in but, Ivor and I bluffed our way in for the afternoon matinees. We thought that we were being very daring.

The Whitehall Theatre in Soho had Peek-a-boo reviews where Phyllis Dixie would perform her striptease act. The troops would queue for hours to get in, and it was said that her flashes of flesh boosted morale during the war years. We never let on to our parents that we went to these shows, saying instead that we'd been looking around the shops.

The houses above us, towards the top of Vale Road were larger, and the families who lived there didn't have much to do with us.

In one was a family named Warnett with two daughters, Molly and Jill, both younger than I was. Her husband, Len Warnett, was a lorry driver who worked for the fellmongers across the Botany. Next door to them was a family called Bartholomew. Bob Bartholomew worked on the railway and he was Mrs Warnett's brother.

Mrs Warnett told her daughters not to have anything to do with that Ray Saunders, as he was a troublemaker.

Many years later I was to work with Bob, who was instrumental in my meeting Jill, Mrs Warnett's younger daughter, who was destined to become my wife.

Chapter 5

After my Grandparents moved to Cranbrook, I spent a lot of time with them. This was due to domestic problems, when my mother would take me off with her to stay with them. This meant that I was taken out of school in Tonbridge, and was free to do my own thing until it was discovered, and I was enrolled in a Cranbrook school. It also meant that I lost a lot of schooling. My education came at a more practical level and it taught me about having a work ethic.

The alleyway between Crown Cottage, where Gran and Dusty lived, and the house next door, led to the Post Office yard and depot. This was where the garage and the store were situated.

The maintenance gang consisted of Alf Bignall the foreman, George Pope the driver and Dusty, who was the wireman. I would go with them in the lorry and I enjoyed the excitement of holes being dug and poles being erected and all the different tools and fittings that would be employed. Gran would pack me up a lunch box with lemonade, ham sandwiches and sausage rolls and I would sit in the back of the lorry at lunchtime with the others and feel part of the team. I've never forgotten the flavour of those lunches.

One time, when laying phone lines to a pig farm, there was a big open barn where the sows were being separated from their litters. When piglets are taken away from a sow, she gets very upset. They are big strong animals and they can become very vicious.

This day, one broke loose and came running down the narrow alleyway between the pens towards us. George Pope shouted a warning to us from the other end, and Dusty quickly jumped up onto the partition wall and he pulled me up out of danger.

The foreman was further along the alley and he started running, being pursued by the sow. With the sow gaining on him, he jumped over into a pen full of pigs. When we went down to find him, he was on his hands and knees covered in muck. We all laughed and Dusty said that you could tell which one was Alf because he was wearing his cap.

The house next to us in Crown Cottage, was across the alleyway and had a high wooden fence with a large gate. Our side had the same, that Dusty had constructed from Post Office materials. Mr and Mrs Barden lived there with their daughter Nita who was the same age as me.

She was a tomboy and we would play together and frequently romp around and play tricks on each other. Sometimes I would call to Nita and then hide behind the fence. When she looked through one of the knotholes, I would squirt her with water from an old hand pump. This would cause laughter and some form of retaliation. Hugh Barden was the fire chief in Cranbrook, and he was never seen without a pipe in his mouth. He was to die later from tongue cancer.

Mrs Barden always seemed to be there cooking or making homemade wine. They had no running water and they had to cross the alleyway with buckets to collect water from us. Outside our back door was a large cast iron pump with a long handle, that would bring water up from the well beneath our cottage. I do not know how this arrangement came about, as our cottage had running water at the kitchen sink. I remember frequently hearing the noise of the pump as we sat in the parlour.

On Sunday mornings Dusty would take me with him, down Cranbrook High Street and through an archway between two shops, to the allotments. The sound of the church bells would fill the air and we would work there and gather any vegetables that Gran needed. At twelve noon we would pack up and go to the pub. Dusty would buy me a lemonade and I would watch him playing darts until two p.m. when we'd go home for lunch. This was usually a roast joint with cabbage and roast potatoes, the taste of which I have never forgotten.

Gran took in lodgers from the Post Office one was an engineer called Ron Evans who maintained the telephone exchanges. He got married and they bought a house nearby. They had one daughter, Ann, a year older than me. His wife Elsie would sometimes ask us to dinner. I remember that on their hallway table there was always a bowl of nuts. As we were leaving, I always sneaked a handful and hid them in my pocket.

Sometimes, if Ron was called out in the evening, he would come and take me with him in the van to locate the fault. It was a little Morris two door van with a square bonnet, and with a radiator cap that had a compass fitted on top. It was during the blackout and the two headlights had metal hoods over them, with three small slots for the lights to shine through.

On rainy nights you could hardly see the road in front of you. I recall one night seeing a searchlight pick up a German bomber in its beam as we drove along. It was heading for London. Luckily, it didn't jettison any bombs, although the anti-aircraft guns were pounding away at it.

The telephone exchanges fascinated me with all the relays revolving, and I thought that I'd like to become a telephone engineer.

***

Ron and Dusty were always good for a laugh, and one time when Cranbrook had a fancy-dress parade, they entered for it. At that time there was a comedian and a film star called Will Hay who used to play a school master with his scruffy pupil.

Dusty went to Cranbrook School and he persuaded the headmaster to lend him his mortarboard hat and gown and a swishy cane. Ron was dressed in shorts with wrinkled socks, an ill-fitting jacket and a schoolboy cap carrying a catapult. They entered as Will Hay and pupil. We watched them come down the High Street in the parade and we had a good laugh. It was in the local newspaper, but I don't think they won a prize.

There was a dance at the Vestry Hall to raise funds for the British Legion, and we all went. Everyone got very jolly and towards the end of the evening, Dusty couldn't resist going up on stage and entertaining the revellers. When the local paper came out, there was a report saying that the dance had been a great success, raising ninety pounds for the cause.

It said that the Vestry Hall had been decorated for the occasion and the Grosvenor Band provided music for the one hundred and twenty dancers.

'A voluntary cabaret turn that met with hearty applause was an exhibition of the sailor's hornpipe by a fine old English gentleman in the person of Mr. H.G. ("Dusty") Rhodes'.

In 1938 the Regal Cinema opened in the Cranbrook High Street just opposite our cottage and Gran used to take me there in the evenings. She loved George Formby and we would always go to watch his films. During the war he made comedy films which were designed to lift people's spirits during the grim times that prevailed. Gran was never one to bother with fashion and she would walk across to the cinema in her carpet slippers.

***

When I was older, I would go to work for a farmer called Mr Love. He had a mixed farm and I remember him putting me to work hoeing a field of turnips. There were long rows of them stretching across this field, and to make it worse, the sheep in the next field kept coming across to eat the turnip tops. Mr Love was paying me threepence an hour and I thought that this meant that I had to work non-stop while he was paying me.

Some days there would be a dogfight going on overhead, but I didn't have much time to watch, being too busy hoeing the turnip rows and chasing the sheep.

At sheep dipping time I used to stand at the end of the row of hurdles that the sheep were being driven down. As they came down, I would open the gate to let one through, so that Mr Love could catch it and dip it. They used to struggle as he tried to get them into the dipping pit. One time a sheep barged past me while the farmer was still bending over, holding a sheep down, and it knocked him flying. He didn't fall right into the pit, but enough to soak him. The Love family were very religious, but I heard him swear that day.

When we were haymaking, Mr Love would work building the stack, and as the hay wagons came round, they would throw each bale to me, and I would pass it to him, to build up the stack. When we got towards the top, I would stand on top of the ladder and catch the straw bales, and he would then thatch the haystack with them. In the afternoon Mrs Love would come out with baskets of sandwiches and lemonade for all of us.

At the end of haymaking, I took my pay packet home and I showed Gran that I'd earned threepence an hour and a bonus of ninepence for each haystack.

Dung spreading was another activity I worked on with them. The farm used heavy horses; there were no tractors. These horses would pull the dung carts and as they went along, we would pitchfork the dung, spreading it over the fields. These carts were made to tip up and were held down by a metal pin that passed through a steel hasp that stuck up from the chassis. When the time came to tip the last of the dung out, this pin was withdrawn and the cart would tip up, so that the men could empty it.

One day, as I was clearing the pinhole with my head under the tipped-up cart, the men had finished, and with no weight to keep it up, the cart came back down onto me. It knocked my head down onto the upturned steel spigot. Luckily this missed my front teeth, but it went up between them and my top lip, ripping the skin. I had to go back to the farmhouse where Mrs Love cleaned it up and sent me home. By the time I'd got home, my lip was black and blue and was swollen up to my nose.

When Gran came home from the school where she was a cleaner, she nearly had a fit and she said that I must go to the doctors. I would not go, but instead I went down to the chemist shop and they sold me a bottle of TCP. After some weeks using this, my lip returned to normal, and I've sworn by TCP ever since.

It meant that my job as a farm worker had ended. Sometime later Mr Love met Dusty in the street. He was employing some students and he said to Dusty that the seventeen-year olds were no use.

He said, "Your grandson can come and work for me any time."
I was thirteen years old.

***

When Dusty approached the Post Office retirement age of sixty, he suffered from high blood pressure and he had a spell off work. He was worried that he would not get his pension. However, he went back, and he finished out his time and he qualified.

The doctor told him that he wasn't to go up ladders again, but this did not deter him. In his spare time, he'd been helping a bloke with a one-man window cleaning business. This man wanted to give it up, so Dusty bought the business from him. I used to help him, and he said that I could have ten percent of all we made. I used to keep a book and Gran said that for the first time she then knew what he earned. We would clean the shop windows in Cranbrook High Street and also the pubs. Dusty would leave me cleaning the outsides, while he did the insides. When I'd finished, I would go in and find him playing darts.

I remember cleaning the outside window of a sports shop and in the window was a cricket bat. I'd never had a proper cricket bat and I wanted to buy it. It was sixteen shillings (80p.) and Mr Croucher the owner, said that he would put it aside for me and I could pay him in instalments. I paid him half a crown a week until it was mine.

Queen Wilhelmina of the Netherlands came to England, where she would do radio broadcasts to the Dutch resistance during the German occupation of Holland. She had bought a large house near Cranbrook and Dusty got the contract to clean the windows inside and out. It took us a week for which we were paid five pounds.

Gran began to worry that it was getting to much for him and she persuaded Dusty to give it up and sell the business. However, this did not stop him from working. I remember him taking on several jobs including cleaning the town lavatories (he got the job after telling the town mayor that they were 'putrefying'). He also cleaned the Post Office exchange, and the boys' school, while Gran cleaned the girls' school. This did not prevent us from hop picking during the season. Gran and I would share a bin and Dusty would go 'pole pulling'.

What I enjoyed most was when he took me cherry picking. We both had old bicycles and we would set off each day to the orchards. Gran would pack up our lunch of sandwiches, sausage rolls and homemade lemonade, and this was placed in a small attaché case and tied onto Dusty's carrier.

On the way, we had to go through a kissing gate. With my smaller bike I could manoeuvre it through without getting off. Dusty would struggle with his bigger bike and one day he got stuck. He tried to get off, but just as he was cocking his leg over, the bike fell sideways, and he fell into the hedge. When we got home and I told Gran, we all had a good laugh. However Dusty was still athletic in his sixties and he could still vault over a five-bar gate.

Cherry trees then were very large and tall. To pick the cherries you had to use long ladders. These were up to twenty-seven feet long, made of wood and very heavy. We were paid by the bushel and our favourites were the 'naps', large black cherries and very juicy. When we were up in the trees picking them, I could hear Dusty going 'puth, puth' as he spat out the stones. I enjoyed them too.

The chargehand of the orchard told Dusty that he doubted my ability to handle the ladders, but I demonstrated that I was strong enough to cope, so he let me pick. We used to pick into large canvas bags hung around our shoulders. The best cherry bunches were often far out on flimsy branches, and to reach them with the ladder was quite precarious.

One day while overreaching, the ladder slipped and fell away from the tree. As it was falling, I jumped off and I rolled over as I landed on the grass, and I wasn't hurt. It taught me to always pitch the ladder into the tree, so that if it slipped that it fell forwards against the trunk. There was no Health and Safety in those days.

When we finished the picking at night, Dusty would fill the attaché case with cherries when no one was looking and tie it onto his carrier. We had to ride out past the charge hand's hut and over a cattle grid. Dusty would shout out goodnight, and riding behind him, I could hear the cherries rattling. Gran loved them and she would make cherry pies.

Chapter 6

When I returned to Tonbridge I returned to school, but my education had suffered, and I struggled to catch up. My parents still hadn't resolved their differences and they told me that they were going to split up. I was asked to choose which one I wanted to go with. I became very upset, and I remember my mother taking me to the home of a teacher called Mr Bishop (Bish) to ask if he could help.

He suggested that I joined the Boy Scouts to help me to cope with my depression. I was duly joined, and I went several times, but I found it all very childish with badges for this and that, and games in the scout hut. I soon dropped out and my parents did not actually separate, although they never really lived in harmony.

The other boys and girls in our road were all older than I was. We sometimes went to a girl's house, whose parents were at work, and we played a game called 'postman's knock' The boys could choose a girl and the winners would get to go into the broom cupboard together. I used to choose Rose, a buxom sixteen-year-old and a very passionate kisser.

***

Years later I had my suits made at Burtons, the men's outfitters in the High Street. The under manager was Johnny Diplock who used to measure me. We became quite friendly and he told me that he and his wife did a singing act in their spare time. One day I happened to meet them, and I was surprised to see that his wife was Rose from the broom cupboard.

***

Food rationing had begun in 1940. Each person had a weekly allowance of one egg, one ounce of cheese, eight ounces of sugar, four rashers of bacon and four ounces of Margarine. Some form of bread rationing was also introduced. Vegetables weren't rationed as they could be home grown. People were encouraged to use every available piece of ground to make a vegetable plot. There was a slogan — 'Dig for Victory'.

Thinking back, I realize that there wasn't the obesity problem that is so prevalent today. Petrol was in short supply for people who had cars, and things like kitchen utensils and even razor blades were difficult to come by, as was timber.

Clothes rationing came in 1941 and coupon books were issued to obtain clothing and shoes. Another slogan was 'Make do and Mend'. Old barrage balloon material, and silk from parachutes from German pilots who had been shot down, could be bought on the black market. This was used to make women's undies (although you could not get elastic), and wedding dresses for wartime brides.

The main reason for food rationing was because Hitler's U Boats were blockading the Atlantic and sinking our convoys. Apart from depriving us of guns and munitions that were coming from America, he was also intent on starving us into submission. Some forms of rationing continued until 1954.

We could buy such things as egg powder off ration. This was a yellow powder that when mixed into a paste with water, could be fried to make a rubber-like omelette. Tins of spam were also sometimes obtainable. The government introduced whale meat, though where that came from, I do not know. My mother would fry me whale steaks that smelt like fish and tasted like fishy meat. Neither of my parents would eat it, but I thought that it would help build me up.

Anything that was not rationed, but in short supply, the shopkeeper would keep under the counter. This reminds me of a joke.

A little boy saw his mother in the bath and pointing to between her legs he asked, "What's that Mum?"

She replied, "That's my nerve." She then said, "I'm going painting later and I want you to go down to the shop and get me a tuppenny brush, and if the man says he hasn't got one, tell him that I want one from under the counter."

The little boy goes to the shop and tells the man that he wants a tuppenny brush, to which the man says that he has not got one.

So, the boy says, "My mum said that she wants one from under the counter."

"Blimey," says the man. "Your mums got a nerve."

"Yes," says the boy, "and I bet it's got more hairs round it than your tuppenny brush."

* * *

By May 1940, Belgium had already given up the fight. This left the British Expeditionary Force cut off, and they had to fight a rearguard action to the coast. They were bottled up for a week under bombardment from the Germans and constant air attack from the Luftwaffe.

At Dunkirk, during the six-day evacuation, we suffered many casualties, but the miracle was that three hundred and sixty thousand troops were brought home by the Royal Navy, with help from a flotilla of little ships that had volunteered. Many of these troops landed at Dover and trains brought them past Tonbridge.

These troops were hungry and exhausted, and the women went to the station to give them cups of tea and what food they could spare. I remember standing with a small crowd that had gathered by the bridge at the top of our road. The women scrambled up to the trains with refreshments. Us children would call out for souvenirs. We learned to shout "avez-vous des souvenir" as many of them were French. The troops would throw down French and Belgian coins, hat badges, bullets and even bayonets and tin helmets. These were then bartered between us. I remember getting a French helmet that I later traded for another air rifle.

France capitulated and declared Paris an open city, allowing the Germans to march in unopposed. Vichy France was set up under Marshall Petain. Apart from some opposition from the French underground resistance, the Nazis ruled Europe. It was expected that they would shortly stage an invasion on us.

Winston Churchill broadcast that we stood alone and that we "must expect the full weight of the enemy to be thrown against us." His speech, incorporating the words, "We will defend our island — we will fight on the beaches — we will NEVER surrender," is famous. His wartime

55

speeches galvanised the nation and they inspired in us the will and the determination to carry on.

Shortly after that, we were fighting for survival in the skies. The Battle of Britain began in July 1940 and it continued until the end of October. I would sometimes stand looking up at the dogfights as our fighters engaged the enemy.

On September the seventh, wave after wave of German bombers and fighters came over. It was reported that there were a thousand in all. Watching them at altitude, the bombers looked black and the smaller fighters showed up as silver. These would break away from the main formations when our fighter planes appeared. The rattle of machine gun and cannon fire could be heard, and the empty cases would drop, sometimes hitting our roof. People watching would cheer if one was shot down unless, as sometimes happened, it was one of ours. When a German pilot bailed out the farm workers would try to get to him first, to confiscate his parachute.

When Hermann Göring realized that he could not defeat the RAF in daylight raids, he switched the attacks to night-time bombing. During the height of the blitz, we would sometimes stand outside at night, and watch the red glow of London burning.

During the air raids I slept in the 'coalhole' under the stairs, on an old piece of coconut matting on top of the coal, and an old eiderdown, together with our mongrel dog Bruce. This was because it was considered to be the safest place, as when you saw a bombed-out building, the stairs were usually the only thing left standing. Both my parents would sit in their armchairs and when things got close, they would dive under the kitchen table.

When the air raids lessened, we would sleep upstairs, and we would only get up if it got bad. We had already been issued with a bucket and a stirrup pump, and a bucket of sand. This was to be used to put out the fires caused by the German incendiary bombs. Some daylight raids continued but these were usually spasmodic with smaller numbers of aircraft.

I continued at the Sussex Road Boys School that was situated near the railway marshalling yards. This was a target for the German Luftwaffe and classes would sometimes be interrupted when the sirens sounded, and we were marched off without haste to the brick-built shelters in the playground. There was no electric light or heating and we sat on wooden forms. The teacher would read to us by the light of an oil lamp.

One day the sirens hadn't sounded when a German bomber suddenly dropped a stick of bombs, obviously trying for the railway yards, but instead hitting a house close to the school, blowing out our classroom windows. The next bomb missed the railway and it demolished a house in the next road. Railway workers lived there, and I think that a driver's wife was killed. We then marched out to the shelters and waited for the 'all clear'.

These attacks became less frequent and school returned to normality. There were shortages though, and I remember that we ran out of writing paper. We were given old exercise books and we tore out the pages and wrote across the existing writing.

I was hopeless at History, Music, Art and most other subjects except for Geography and Mental Arithmetic. Geography involved a lot of drawing, which I was good at and I enjoyed.

About this time there was a 'wings for victory' week, where you were invited to send in slogans to the local newspaper to win a prize. The government was selling saving stamps to fund the war, and my slogan was — 'Saving brings Victory wings'. It won first prize. However, I was upset when they published it as — 'Savings bring Victory wings' with the s in the wrong place it spoilt the slogan.

I also entered the Daily Herald competition for strip cartoons, and I had two published and I received postal orders for two shillings and sixpence.

We had gardening lessons given by a Mr Chasmer. I remember him describing double digging which was called 'bastard trenching'. We had to pronounce it as 'bass-tard'. I found this amusing. Each of us was allotted a small plot of ground where we grew vegetables and had some currant bushes.

It wasn't unusual for me to get into trouble with the teachers for larking about or being cheeky. 'Bish' would only throw a piece of chalk at you to pay attention or give you a smack across your buttocks with an old gym slipper.

The Maths and R.E. teacher, Mr Stonely, was more of a disciplinarian and he would rap you across the knuckles with a ruler or send you to the headmaster's office for a caning.

Mr Fletcher was a sadistic character who enjoyed waving a long swishy cane about. He would use it to whack your outstretched fingers. To receive your strokes meant waiting outside his office until he was ready.

This had its compensations, as his secretary was a good-looking girl of about twenty-two. She was the daughter of Jones the High Street jeweller. Miss Jones would sit behind a table facing the door, and if you were first in the queue you could look through the open door and see up her skirt. I sometimes thought that having six of the best was worth it.

I enjoyed the sports lessons and I played cricket and football. I was also good at P.E. and I particularly enjoyed diving over the vaulting horse.

Once a week, we would go to a workshop to be taught woodwork and metalwork. I made several things, and for my woodwork test, I made a trinket box and a picture frame which I still have. We would also be taken to a hall to learn dancing, with the girls from an adjoining school. The dancing teacher was a striking woman with shapely legs, big calves and an ample bosom. If you could not master the steps, she would take hold of you and tell you to follow her body movements. I found the closeness of her body very stimulating, and I would funk the steps, so that she would grab me and get me to press my legs against hers to dance.

By this time, my father had been selected for a promotion. He was transferred to the railway surveyors' department offices to become a Chainman. This entailed his working on bridge and tunnel surveys.

I was struck down with Bronchial pneumonia and I was ill in bed for several weeks. A doctor Houston came and prescribed a course of M&B tablets, an early form of antibiotics. They said that it saved my life.

After that I became very interested in physical fitness and I joined the Health and Strength League. I saw an advert for the Charles Atlas course, and I ordered it. He was an American who published an exercise routine called 'Dynamic Tension'. Each fortnight, he would send a new routine which had to be progressively followed. It involved various exercises but without weights.

Another task was to take a cold shower every morning by an open window. We had no such facility, so I would take a bowl of cold water up to my bedroom and I would sponge myself down in front of the open window. I'm not sure now what it was supposed to do for you, but it was certainly invigorating in the winter.

It was costing me two shillings and sixpence a fortnight for these programmes, so I thought of a way to make a profit from them. In the surveyors' office where Dad worked, they had a copying machine. I got him to copy me off a dozen or so copies each time, and I sold them for sixpence each to the other boys at school.

I was always bartering or trading things with other boys. I also bought rough castings of model aircraft made from an alloy, and then I'd file and polish them before mounting them on alloy ash trays. I'd take them to school and sell them. I remember that the Spitfire and Mosquito were the most popular. I had quite a following, and I also gave protection to some of the weaker boys, from the school bullies. They were always willing to buy what I had to sell.

My main enjoyment came from going to the cinema. Hilda Cosham, who lived along the road, had a friend named Eileen and they both became usherettes at the Ritz Cinema. I used to arrange to be outside the fire exit at a certain time, and they would let me in and sneak me into the best seats.

When I was recovering from the bronchial infection, the doctor let me get up to go and see a film called 'Cover Girl' starring Gene Kelly and Rita Hayworth. I had never seen such beauty and I instantly fell in love with her.

These American films introduced me to a world that I never realised existed, with lovely apartments, fridges and shower rooms, and it strengthened my determination to one day achieve such luxury.

There was a boathouse and a landing stage by the Cannon Lane bridge on the Medway River. This was where the boys from Tonbridge School had their rowing boats.

They could often be seen rowing down the river, with their coach riding his bicycle along the tow path, as he shouted instructions through a megaphone. When they weren't there, Les Cosham and some other boys used to swim there. He took me and he taught me to swim. He would dive in and then get me to jump in towards him and to keep making the strokes with my arms. At first, I would go under, but I soon learned to kick my legs and stay afloat. Pretty soon I was swimming, and I particularly enjoyed running and diving in.

Mum knitted me my first pair of trunks. She used wool, and they would fill up with water and finish up around my ankles when I dived in.

There was a five-foot wall that ran down to the jetty and we would dive off it. The water was always murky, and as there was a submerged fence under the water, it was important to make sure that you dived far enough out to avoid it. Sometimes we would swim up to the town bridge past the gas works. There were big pipes emptying the effluent from the works into the river. This was green and smelt of sulphur. Often, there would be dead fish, belly up, as you swam through it.

***

I had never taken the eleven plus exam, but when I was fourteen there were three free places offered for the Tunbridge Wells Technical College. I took the test and I was then sent for an oral exam in front of three judges. They asked me questions, some of which I could not answer.

Then one asked what my father did. I said that he was a railway Chainman. He then asked if he ever spoke to me about his work and I said no. He asked me if I knew what measurements surveyors used. I'd heard of rods, poles, perches and chains so I said those. Then he asked if I knew anything more and I said no. He then asked me what a chain is usually made up of, and I replied links.

His face lit up and he turned to the other judges and they said, "That will be all." About a week later a letter came to say that I'd been accepted.

The course I'd chosen was Draughtsmanship, as I thought that it would involve a lot a drawing, which I was good at. However, there wasn't much, and I found the teacher boring. The good thing was that we would all go to the indoor swimming pool in Monson Road. I remember that it was heavily chlorinated, and the fumes hung heavily over the water. When leaving, my eyes would be bloodshot.

The best part was that they had an army cadet force. Fully equipped in khaki battledress, we would go to an army depot in Southborough where we would drill. Some days we went to the firing range where we fired Lee Enfield .303 rifles. Being left-handed, I found it difficult to operate the bolt action, but I enjoyed the shooting. Some evenings I would don on my uniform and go to the cinema feeling like a real soldier. I used to think that it attracted the attention of the girls.

After six months I had enough of the boring lessons, so I left. There was a two-pound penalty for this as it denied another boy of the opportunity. When I told my parents that it was necessary to pay a two-pound penalty, they said that I would have to find the money, so I did odd jobs till I'd earned enough to leave.

***

When writing this account of my life, I was searching through some old photos and I came across a bundle of old letters. These had been sent to me during the troubled periods of my parent's marriage. Some were from Gran and Dusty to me in Tonbridge, and some were to my mother. I've included a condensed version of some of them here, as they give an insight into life during the war and our family problems at the time. These letters were written in pencil on scrap paper.

September 1936

Written by my mother to me in Cranbrook around my seventh birthday. She is sending me a book that I'd ordered. She refers to me receiving money from her to buy an airgun. She says that Dad would get me some pellets when he went to Maidstone. Mum was a cleaner at the Baa, Baa factory in Vale Road and she had told Gran that she could be made forewoman because of her good work.

9 January 1937

I was seven years and four months old. Dusty wrote to "Mabel" (Mum) that Gran had the face-ache and that she was going to have her other teeth out. He hoped that her head was better. (I remember that my mother frequently suffered from headaches).

10 June 1938

I was eight years and nine months old. Dusty wrote to Mabs (Mum) that mother (Gran) was going to Maidstone shopping and that he was going to meet her with Ron (Ron Evans who lodged with them). He wrote, "If I can't write I can play darts and I have never been beaten in Tonbridge." He hoped that Ray was being a good boy.

12 October 1938

I was nine years old. Dusty was fifty-eight and suffering from high blood pressure and angina.

To me, he wrote that he was getting better and he hoped to start work the next week. He said that he was pleased to hear that I could write better than he did. He said that if he couldn't write that he could play darts.

He said, "If you keep going on as you are, you will soon get a foreman's job on the telephone. Uncle Alf said that he would be glad when you could come to Cranbrook, so he could leave you in charge again."

Prior to that, I had written an undated letter to Mum and Dad (without joined up writing), saying that I had arrived safely and that I had been through the woods with Grandpop. Also, that I was going to work with Grandpop in the lorry to Tenterden.

"Gran is packing me up some 'sosijous', a leg of chicken and lemonade.

"Love Raymond xxxxxxxx."

18 September 1939

I was one day away from my tenth birthday. Dusty wrote to Mum that he had made it up with Gran and that he was sorry to have upset Mum and me and he asked to be forgiven. He said that they were the best of pals and he asked whether Mum would write her a nice letter to cheer her up, as she didn't like to see Mum and me going away like that.

8 December 1939

I was ten years and three months old. Dusty wrote to me, saying that Gran was sending my Christmas box as they wouldn't be home (Tonbridge) for Christmas. He said that he would be seeing me sometime after Christmas and that I was to be a good boy — but he said that I was always good.

11 October 1942

I was thirteen years old. Dusty wrote to Mum that he was pleased to see that 'Nibo' (he used to refer to me as 'Nibo' and Gran used to keep my savings book for me) gave Gran all that money to bring back. It will help his book a lot He went on to say, "Tell Jim I shan't have no more cider till I see him again then I shall have a lot to get back."

13 October 1942

Dusty wrote to Mabs. He ordered a tame rabbit for Xmas and he said that she should look for another job.

26 October 1942

I was thirteen years and one month old. Dusty wrote to Mum, saying that he wanted a pushbike so that he could bike home to Tonbridge and not catch the bus. Although they had moved to Cranbrook years before, Gran and Dusty always referred to Tonbridge as home.

He wrote, "Ask Nibo to look for one in Tonbridge, as I cannot get one in Cranbrook."

He complained that the schoolwork (the caretaking) was too much for them and that if they could not get someone to help with the workload that he was handing in his notice. He wanted someone to do Miss Porter's work, so that they only had the big school to do.

He said, "Tell Nibo not to be out of pocket making them toys, they will have to pay for them out of the shops. P.S. Tell Jim that if I get a bike, I shall be riding home on the handlebars if I get about seventeen pints of cider in me, and I shall be able to fight the German army single handed."

7 November 1942

Dusty wrote to Mabel — hoping that they would find a new man for the school job. He said, "Roll on hopping so that Nibo can be with them again."

6 December 1942

I was thirteen years and three months old. Dusty wrote thanking me for the 2/6 (two shillings and sixpence) postal order that I sent him. He had left the school caretaker job.

He was trying to buy another window cleaning business as there wasn't enough for him with what he had in Cranbrook. He was sixty-two years old. He told me to keep the toy business going and to roll in the money.

He had referred to hop picking the previous summer, when I had been staying with them in Cranbrook. He was glad that Mum had been appointed forewoman Saunders. (That would have been at the Baa, Baa factory where they were making leather gilets for the army).

11 April 1943

I was thirteen years and seven months old and Dusty was sixty-three.

He wrote to me, saying that he was much better (he'd been unable to work) and he thanked me for sending him "the bacca" and the ten shillings. He was pleased to hear that I had passed one of my exams and he hoped that I would pass the other one as it would help me a lot in life. He said that they were coming home at Easter and that they were going to aunt Fan's place (Aunt Fan is Gran's sister, who had remarried and lived in Tonbridge). He said that I could go back with them and stay for the week.

15 June 1943

Dusty wrote to me, saying, "I beat the record today. I picked four and I made up the other baskets that made me one pound today, so look sharp and come out again. I have missed you today, you are a great help to me. Hope to see you again on Friday night and we will show 'em."

He must have been referring to cherry picking.

28 November 1943

Dusty wrote to me, saying that he was in bed with a bad cold. He was glad that my leg was a lot better. This referred to an accident that I had when I was staying with them. I was alone and sitting in an armchair reading a Sexton Blake novel, with a toffee bar on my lap. I could not break the toffee so I took out my pocketknife and I used the point to stab through the toffee bar. It went straight through and it penetrated deep into my thigh.

I pulled it out, but I could not stop the bleeding. I took a wet flannel and I went to bed, clutching the flannel to the wound. When my Grandparents came home, they asked me what I'd done, and they pleaded with me to go to the doctors. I would not go, and eventually the bleeding stopped, and the wound gradually healed over. But it should have been stitched, as it grew apart, with a scar that is still visible today.

17 January 1944

Dusty wrote that he had cleaned the exchange windows that day but that he hadn't got the exchange job yet. That was the caretaker and cleaning job at the telephone exchange.

21 May 1944

Dusty wrote to me. "I'm glad you like your job, it's better than going to school."

He told me that he was going to a sale three times that week (he used to go as a porter) and that if he saw any wire netting that he would get it for me.

The job that he referred to was when I left the technical collage to work on the railway.

An undated letter from Gran spoke of Dusty going to a sale for three days the week before but he hadn't bought anything as it was all antiques.

But there was another sale on the seventh of June. This letter referred to me asking her if Derek Swan and I could go and stay with them for the weekend. We used to cycle there.

***

Tonbridge had a Prisoner of War Camp at Somerhill that was set up soon after the outbreak of World War Two.

In October 1942, General Montgomery launched the second battle of El Alamein in the desert, resulting in the capture of thirty thousand German and Italian troops. Some of them were imprisoned there.

In the years following, they were let out to work on the farms and I remember them walking about the town in POW uniforms with a dark blue circle sewn on the back. At the camp they made jewellery and rings from pieces of scrap metal and Perspex.

Women and girls would stand outside the camp and barter cigarettes for these items. Fraternisation took place and after the war a number of them married English girls and settled here.

***

My father heard of a job in the Signal and Telegraph Department of the railway. The office boy had been called up and there was a vacancy (as it happens, he was Jill's cousin and he went into the RAF and served out the war as an air gunner). His mother, Jill's auntie Floss, was the office cleaner (the inspector used to call her the old biddy).

I got the job and I sat at a desk opposite Sub Inspector Herbert Jennings. He was a dapper little man and when we were alone, he would mimic the inspector and joke about him.

The Inspector was a big old boy, Jack Edwards, who had been a sergeant in France in the First World War. He was a stickler for doing everything by the book and he would visit the gangs every day to see that the work was being carried out properly.

When the two of them walked out together they were referred to as Mutt and Jeff. I got on well with both of them. Mr Jennings helped me to improve my writing and my spelling. There were no typewriters. Everything was done in long hand. The inspector, Mr Edwards sat at a separate desk to my right.

The Southern Railway had many different departments that were responsible for every aspect of its operations. Just next to Tonbridge Station was the goods yard in Vale Road and sidings where the trucks would be shunted to link up into freight trains.

On the opposite side of the tracks, down Priory Road, were the loco sheds, the coal yards and up at the top end, by the station, were several other departments; The Permanent Way department, Gas and Water, Electricians and our office, the Signal and Telegraph department. We also had a store run by Charlie Smith who always seemed miserable. Our fitters had a workshop and there was a paint store, a carpenter's shop and the Linesmen's shop. The Chief Linesman, Norman Pearson, had a little office adjoining ours. He was a little man nicknamed 'Pidge'.

All of these operational departments were clustered around the station and there were two signal boxes, Tonbridge East and Tonbridge West. There was even a railway police office, with Detective Sergeant Huggett and his sidekick.

All the workforce was male except for our paint shop which had three women painters. There was no such thing as sexual harassment in those days and lots of flirting and banter went on, but the women seemed to enjoy it and they joined in.

I soon settled into the office routine and I was given various documents, order forms and letters to copy out in long hand. It wasn't long before I was ordering supplies from our head office in Wimbledon and as the inspector gained confidence in me, he would leave it to me to deal with internal memos.

When he got letters from head office wanting details of work that had been carried out, he would hand them to me and say, "Write a story 'round it boy."

I could even make a good copy of his signature. Little did head office know that their queries were being answered by a fifteen-year-old office boy!

The letters from head office in Wimbledon would come down by train to the goods office in Vale Road. On my way to work, I would go through the ticket barrier at the station, and down to the goods office. After collecting the mail, I would cross to the 'up' platform then walk down under the bridge where the branch line from Hastings ran through. I'd then cross the rails to where our offices were. This was not without danger as you could not see any approaching trains until they were almost upon you.

I would also be given the task of making out all the time sheets, and later they would take me with them to site meetings where a new signal gantry was to be installed. Back at the office I would draw out the plans and fill out the work application forms.

The working week was forty-eight hours. Monday to Friday, from seven thirty a.m. till five p.m. with a lunch break of half an hour, plus Saturday mornings from eight a.m. till noon. On Fridays, we finished at four p.m. and we collected our pay.

A clerk from the station ticket office would come down to the office next to ours, and everyone would queue at the window for their pay packet. This was paid every week by cash and one week in arrears. There were only two days holiday with pay, Good Friday and Christmas day.

You were entitled to one week's paid holiday a year, after you had completed a full year's service.

There was an old railway carriage situated by the goods yard, and every Wednesday night a local GP would come and give us first aid lessons. We were taught to bandage wounds, treat injuries and fix splints. Being the junior, I was often used as the guinea pig.

Sometimes the inspector would send me down to our depot at Eastbourne with items that they required, and this gave me the freedom to travel around by train.

I remember one afternoon on the way back, I spotted a German bomber from the window that had seen the train and was circling above. I felt very vulnerable and helpless, fearing an attack. Luckily, one of our fighters turned up and chased it off. I heard the rattle of machine gun fire, but the train continued, and I did not see the outcome.

The railway had its own branch of the Home Guard and they would gather together after work to drill and get instructions. My father hated it, as he had a dislike for the officer, who was a member of the Permanent Way Department

There was quite a bit of indiscipline. Our Chief Linesman was made sergeant and his office was used to store the weaponry. There were three rifles, a Smith and Wesson revolver, a Sten gun, some grenades and ammunition. I was given the job of keeping the logbook updated with the current arsenal.

After I'd been there about a year, I was given the chance to learn about the signalling and the telephone work and I joined the linesman, George Bedford, at our Sevenoaks depot. My office job was taken over by the son of the Permanent Way inspector. Their office adjoined ours and the Inspector, Ron Santer and his sub, Burt Turk, both lived above us in Vale Road.

George was a convivial man and he took me under his wing. He always seemed in a hurry and he used to walk very fast. While waiting for our train one morning, he took me to the station buffet and bought us tea. I was anxious in case the inspector came in and found us drinking tea. One day he did, but after nodding to us, he merely had a cup himself. I was surprised to find that this was accepted as part of the working day, as long as you did not stay too long.

My father was working on bridge and tunnel surveys with a young surveyor named Pete Beretta. He was Swiss and he had a sister who was married to Fred Hurdle. Fred was a tough character, who when drunk, was apt to pick fights. Pete owned a beach chalet at Dungeness in Kent that had been requisitioned for the Army.

When it was no longer needed, the government released it, and Pete, with his sister and Fred, would go down at weekends to paint and repair it. I was invited to join them, and we would go down and stay there from Friday night till Sunday. Pete had a little Hillman saloon and he could get petrol from the railway.

I remember how his sister used to cook big full English breakfasts, and I was then given the job of painting the outside.

After lunch, I would go down to the beach and swim off the point. It was all pebbles and very steep. When the tide was in, the water was very deep. Getting out one day I looked back and I saw several large conger eels that had followed me in. They were about six feet long and as big around as my thighs. After that, I was very wary, and I never swam out too far.

One Sunday on the way home, we stopped off at a pub and after several drinks Fred got into an argument and a fight broke out. He smashed a chair and then broke a pint glass against the counter and threatened a bloke with it. There was an ugly scene, but luckily Pete managed to calm things down and we left without much harm done. It rather spoilt things and when I told my father he advised me not to go again.

***

Dad was a good billiards player and he would sometimes take me to a billiards hall in Tunbridge Wells where he taught me to play. This was near to Calverley Road where he used to work. Opposite was a motorcycle shop run by Bill Jury. I saw a second-hand Triumph 350 Speed Twin in the window one day and I decided to buy it. It was maroon with a modern nacelle headlamp and instrument panel, and a sprung hub rear wheel. I loved it.

I soon learned to ride, and I took my test in Tunbridge Wells. On the day of the test I reported to the testing office, and the testing officer asked me questions and filled out the form. Then he took me out onto the road, and he asked me to ride up and down so that he could watch me. Lastly, he said that he wanted me to ride up to the traffic lights and circle around the roads where he would be watching. He said that somewhere on the route he would step out in front of me, and I was to make an emergency stop. I kept circling around, but I never saw him.

After about twenty minutes I got fed up and I went back to the office. I told the other chap what I'd been doing, and I asked where the examiner had got to.

He said, "Oh, he's been taken to hospital."

He had stepped out in front of someone else, and they'd knocked him down. I don't think that he was seriously hurt, but at any rate they passed me.

***

On 6 June 1944 the allied forces landed in Normandy, and the battle began, to liberate France and get to Berlin. I remember standing and looking up at the many aircraft, some towing gliders, that were heading for the coast to join the battle. The Dakota aircraft and the gliders had large white stripes painted on their wings. I wished that I was old enough to be with them, as I always felt frustrated at being on the receiving end and never being able to fight back.

One foggy morning several days later, as we were preparing to go to work, my father and I were puzzled by what seemed to be a succession of low flying aircraft passing overhead. They seemed very low and the noise from their engines was very loud, like an engine without an exhaust. I went to our back door and I looked up but I could not see anything because of the mist. Then I noticed my father, who had been in the outside lavatory, on his hands and knees peering around the door.

As we walked up the road to work, people were saying that it was a new jet plane that we had invented. As the fog lifted, however, we could see that they were in fact large bombs with a pointed nose, short stubby wings and a jet engine mounted on top. The noise they made was very distinctive and we were soon to learn that when the engine stopped, a few seconds later there would be an explosion.

In the days that followed, I would watch them as they passed overhead, but if the engine cut out as it was approaching, it meant diving for cover. These were the V1 flying bombs, and we nicknamed them doodlebugs. They were launched from the French coast towards London as they had a limited range. The bomb contained 2300 lbs of high explosive but it could not be directed at a specific target. Many were intercepted by our fighters, and those that got through had to pass the ring of anti-aircraft guns and barrage balloons protecting the Capital.

One time as I stood watching, I saw one strike the tethering cable of a balloon, and it spun around and came back. On another occasion, I saw a Spitfire chase one as it headed in the direction of the town. The Spitfire flew alongside it and tipped its wing over, causing it to plummet to the ground exploding in a field. The story at the time was that Neville Duke, a fighter pilot ace, whose mother lived in Tonbridge, had done it. I doubt whether this is true, but it was good for morale.

Life went on as normal, both at work and in pleasure. Once, while in the cinema, I heard one approaching and when the engine cut out, I held my breath for the few seconds before the explosion came. It was quite close, and it shook the building. Small flakes of plaster floated down from the ceiling through the beam of the projector. The Germans were launching over one hundred a day from the Pas-de-Calais, and in all, some nine and a half thousand were launched; until the allies overran the launching sites. Many of these exploded in Kent, the last at Orpington, and Kent was nicknamed 'bomb alley'.

By September the V1s had stopped but they were followed by the V2 rockets which had a much longer range. It was the first guided ballistic missile, with a range of two hundred miles, travelling at over three thousand mph. They were directed at London, causing many thousands of civilian deaths. There was no warning with these, just the sudden explosion. I didn't witness these close up but I was travelling to Maidstone on the train when one dropped on the goods yard there, killing two railwaymen and the dray horses.

The following is a copy of the letter that Gran had written to me at the time:

'Dear Ray

'Thanks for your letter duck, I was very pleased to get it, and to know that you are all safe.

'What a time we are having, these 'jitter bugs' are awful we get them all day and all night and big explosions all around us. They bring a lot down, but I pity those poor devils who get bombed out. One was brought down over the field beyond Croucher's house, but the blast went Wisley Pound way and damaged a lot of cottages. Some of the ceilings in the school came down. The guns are awful, there are three in the field close to the school and when they open up, I think me, and the school are going up too. They had a meeting to know if they should close the school down, but decided to keep it open, but they can't make the parents send their children to school, so some go, and some stay away.

'Grandad is having a rotten time with his windows. If he is up the ladder he has to come down or the guns would bring him down. Yesterday, he hurt his foot and he could not get down quick enough, you should hear what he calls them.

'He could go cherry picking at the same place as last year, but Jeff next door says it puts the wind up him when the bullets whizz through the trees, so I don't think he will go.

'Benenden has caught it very badly and Hawkhurst. Robin has been blasted twice, had the windows blown out and ceilings down. Well duck I could tell you a lot, but I had better not, or you will say I am helping the enemy. Well duck I am pleased that you still like your work and are sheltered where you work, how does Mum get on at her works. Grandad sends his love and now I must say cheerio and love to you all from Gran. xxxx.'

This letter gives an insight as to how life was during the war. Throughout these attacks, and the earlier blitz, people still carried on going to work. There was a spirit of determination and defiance among the people, probably helped by the fact that most of them; the working classes at any rate, were used to hardship and tough times. This is not to say that the better off didn't also show fortitude. People always seemed to keep cheerful and make light of the dangers and the shortages.

I sometimes wonder how the present generation would cope, being used to an easy life and their belief in their rights, with the entitlement society. I was brought up to believe, that one's only right in life was the right to struggle.

***

The war in Europe ended on 8th May 1945 when Germany surrendered.

Churchill's broadcast to the nation said, "We may allow ourselves a brief period of rejoicing but let us not forget the toil and effort that lies ahead."

Later he stood on the balcony of The Ministry of Health in London and he declared that it was the people's victory. A massive crowd had gathered and cheered him. Despite this, when the General Election came in July he lost. I think this broke the old man's heart. The war with Japan continued until August.

In Tonbridge there were street parties, and a victory parade through the High Street. All kinds of floats on the back of lorries came along, and I stood at the top of Vale Road watching them. Halfway through, a large float with lots of people waving came by, and leading the procession, dancing and singing, was none other than Dusty.

***

Another letter that I found, was one from my mother to me when I was fifteen, after she had left my father and me. She had gone to Cranbrook to live with Gran and Dusty.

She wrote that Dusty was miserable because I had forgotten his birthday. She thought that my dad and I were going to Cranbrook to see them.

She said that I was bloody selfish and that we used to be pals and comrades and that she had only hung on for me. I was all she lived for, when my dad did not want her 'that time', all those months when his interests were elsewhere.

She said that she worshipped me and that she went out to work when I was at school to clothe me and to give me all that she could.

Since I had begun to work, she had let me keep the lion's share, thinking that it would help my bank book so that whatever happened I would have something behind me. Now it was all going on a bloody motorcycle and where had it got her. I took everything as a matter of course instead of looking around to see what other boys' mothers took, yet they still respected their mothers. They wouldn't dream of taking their savings and doing what they liked with them.

I did not even ask her; and would say that I did this or that, as if I were a man and not fifteen years old.

Gran and Dusty realized that they had done too much for me. It hurt them to hear the way that I spoke to my mum. My gran said that some fathers would knock me down if I spoke to them the way that I speak to her. All I wanted her for, was to get me clean shirts etc., and I had told her that I did not want her back and I said that I was okay without her.

My interests were enough for me, and I did not stop to think that she was grieving for a little sign of love from the son who had been her very life.

She'd done everything for me and I just swore and carried on as I wanted to. I'd hurt Dusty, one of the kindest old men who had ever breathed who'd worshipped me from the day I was born.

On the Friday, I had dressed up and gone out for the evening. I would have done better to have spent the money on my grandad, and she did not think that lighting the fire and getting the tea was doing much. She had sold her chicken because I had wanted her garden shed and she hoped that I was satisfied.

It wouldn't hurt me to give up an evening and polish a room for her. It would have helped my dad who's had to do all the washing and ironing and cleaning, and I just let him get on with it. She'd given me everything and I had no respect for her and very little affection.

She reminded me that I owed Dusty a pound and that he had not got it back and he was nearly broke.

She did not expect that she would be coming home again as neither I nor my dad really needed her. She was grateful for all that my dad had done for her while she was ill, as a lot of men would not have done it, but he didn't love her. He would fly into a temper and swear at her, because she had said that the shop bill was high for only two of us for five days, and there had been a row over it.

She had gone to bed and cried all afternoon and he would not go near her. He had gone up to the pub after tea and he had come back ten minutes before his bus left; as if ten minutes was enough to cure all the hurt. All he thought about was his office work and that all he needed was his bed there. Now that his office was being transferred to Ashford, she would see even less of him. She went on to say that we did not need her anymore and that she would look for a job in Cranbrook and not come back as we did not need her.

She said that Gran did not say much and that she would not interfere, but that Gran sided with her. Dusty took my dad's side but he said that if she could not live a happy life, she'd better break their marriage up.

Dusty had told Mum that when Dad went, he had had tears in his eyes and he said, "I'm going home miserable Harry."

But she knew that it wasn't true, as she did not mean that much to him. If he was that miserable, he could have gone upstairs and told her so. When he visited, he had kissed her as though she had leprosy. When he slept there, it was like sleeping with a log. He nursed Bruce the dog and he spoke to him as if butter would not melt in his mouth, but not to her.

Mum said that I only wrote to her the first week she was gone, and we could both sing 'I get along without you very well'. She'd been made to feel that she was not good enough and that we had given her an inferiority complex. She's always loved us with all her heart but she cannot go on being treated that way. When she was settled, she would collect her things but she's not taking the blame for this.

She goes on, to say that we had both shown her that she does not matter much to us. She wouldn't stay there any longer than she can help it, as it worries Gran and Dusty.

She wished to God that she had supported them and never knew that the day would come when she would realise that her son and her husband did not care about her.

She ended the letter, saying, 'That's all my son, it's straight from my heart, but I'll win through yet. God bless you, Mum'.

This is a condensed account of a very long and powerful letter. I found it in the bundle of letters written by Gran and Dusty to me. They were in a box hidden away at the back of the cellar with old photos and things that people accumulate. I have no recollection of having read it at the time and finding it more than seventy years later both shocked and saddened me.

I cannot imagine what effect it must have had on me at the time, as a fifteen-year-old boy. I do remember that she had split with my father and she had gone to live with her parents, and my father and I carried on alone for some time. There had always been rows between my parents.

As a child I would often hear them arguing downstairs and I would creep down and look through the gap above the stair's door. It was usually about him not loving her and seeing another woman.

He would always deny this, but she had found letters in his pockets. How much of this was true or imagined I do not know. I do know that times were hard and that my father had been trapped in a marriage that he could not have wanted.

My mother had been a fun-loving extrovert who loved dancing, whereas my father was of a reserved, rather introverted nature.

Was he unfaithful? I think it's likely that he had an affair with the woman at his office, but it's also true that he stuck by my mother. He certainly looked after her when she was ill, and later when she had treatment for a nervous breakdown.

As for my part in her unhappiness, I can only say that I do recall selfishly wanting to break away from what I had come to realise was a deprived way of living. My frustration was probably responsible for my horrible attitude and my behaviour towards her.

I also remember that at the time, of her depression, I had tried to console her, but she could not or would not be consoled. Attitudes then were very different from todays. People were expected to pull themselves together and shake themselves out of it.

Sometime after that, she returned home to Tonbridge and life resumed amicably, but she still suffered with bouts of depression. A little later we made up, and I have a photo of her riding with me on the back of my motorbike.

***

I became friendly with Dennis Newman who'd gone to school with me. He lived at the other end of town, and he also had a motor bike. We would go around together. His brother Ron was a plumber, and Dennis worked with him and he was earning much more than the railway paid me. He said that I should try for a job on the buildings.

I went to a small building firm run by two brothers named Smith in Lyons Crescent. I asked the person in the office if there was a job going. He said that all he could offer was a job digging out footings for some new bungalows that they were building.

I was sixteen so he only offered me a boy's wages. I insisted that I could work the same as a man and that I wanted a man's wage. He said he'd take me on at a boy's wages for two weeks, and if I could keep up with the men, he would then pay me a man's wage. This suited me, so I left the railway and I started to work for him.

The footings were dug by a gang of Irish labourers on piece work. They worked non-stop but I managed to keep up and I earned the right to be paid a man's wage.

There was a brickyard in Tonbridge and lorries would deliver bricks straight from the kilns, that were still warm. The driver would throw them down five at a time, and you had to catch them by clutching them together. These were stacked in rows ready for the bricklayers, who were also on piece work.

Another piece worker was Harry the plasterer. I was given the job of mixing the Siraphite for him. He had forearms like Popeye from the constant plastering. He worked very fast and sometimes I struggled to keep up with him. If the Siraphite was mixed too stiff, he could not spread it, and if too wet it would form a ripple. I stayed with him till the end but I wasn't sorry when the job was done.

***

When the bungalows were finished, they kept me on, and they put me as a mate to Vic Fry. Vic had been a boiler engineer in the Royal Navy and he worked for them as a plumber. Our first job was to install a new boiler in the David Salomon Home in Southborough. We had to remove the old boiler, which was in large heavy sections, and all the pipe work was wrapped in asbestos padding. We had no protective clothing or masks then, and at night when we had finished, we would look just like snowmen. Asbestosis had not been heard of then.

We were given two bicycles with grid baskets on the front that carried our tools, and we would cycle to houses where plumbing repairs were needed. Pipes were mainly made of lead, and a burst would be repaired by wiping a 'joint' onto it. This was done using a paraffin blowlamp and sticks of solder, that when heated would be wiped around the pipe using a mole skin flannel. If you did not heat it enough the solder would crumble. Too hot and it would melt and drop off.

One day we were working at a house along the Hadlow Road. The woman let us in but then she said that she was going out. There was a burst above the sink, and I asked Vic to let me have a go. I became so engrossed in wiping the joint that I inadvertently held the blowlamp to close to the lace curtain. In an instant it shrivelled up and just hung there like a black cobweb.

I looked for Vic to ask him what I should do, but he was in the larder helping himself to a cold chicken. I said what will the woman say when she comes back.

Vic thought that I meant about the chicken, so he wrapped the skin around it and he said, "She'll never notice."

We left soon after and we never heard any more about it. The good thing was, that the joint that I had wiped was successful.

Any scrap lead, which we called 'bluey', we would take to Butlers, the scrap merchant in Priory Road opposite the coal yard. He would put it on the scales and pay us the going rate. Vic and I would share the proceeds. Old Butler was a scruffy little man and he would drive about the town in a Sunbeam Talbot 90 Sports car, the same as Stirling Moss drove with success in the Monte Carlo Rally. Owning one was another of my ambitions.

Vic liked to bet on the horses, and he took me to the bookies. This was also in Priory Road. Cash betting was illegal, so their premises were always tucked away out of sight.

Bob Bert's office was a little hut behind a row of tenement houses. Old Bob would sit behind the counter with a fag in his mouth. He would hold the phone in one hand while writing down bets with the other, as his 'runners' phoned them in.

Occasionally he would look up and take your money and betting ticket. These would be strewn out along the counter. Behind him was the ticker tape where another man stood making notes of the latest odds and results.

We had to go to a big house that needed a new ball valve for the tank that was in the loft. As Vic was fitting it, he noticed that the lead pipe ran from the tank right around the loft to the far corner. He said that wasn't necessary, so he cut out a long piece and then he joined it up again by pulling it across from the corner.

He overdid it, however, and I strained to hold the two ends together so that he could make the joint. He told me to go down and fetch a sack from our bicycles, we then hid the lead and carried it out with our tools. We took it to Butlers yard, and he paid us fifteen shillings.

Vic fancied a horse that was running that afternoon. It was a short-priced favourite, and he said that it could not lose, it was a certainty. We put the whole fifteen shillings on it to win. Later that day we went back to Bob Bert's to collect our winnings and we found that it had only finished third. That taught me that there is no such thing as a sure thing.

The boss's brother, Peter Smith, was a plumber who installed kitchens and bathrooms. He was a powerful man and very strong. I'd seen him pick up a six-foot cast iron bath, put it over his head and shoulders, and carry it up the stairs. He'd seen me working and he told his brother that I should work with him, so I did, and I learned another branch of the trade.

Shortly after that Dennis Newman was killed on his motor bike in an accident along London Road.

Chapter 7

Higher up the road where I lived, in Vale Road, were the Mitchells. Alec, the youngest son, was a few years older than me and he worked as a trainee fireman on the railway. We began going around together.

Alec would often start a sentence by saying, "I've got a snakey feeling."

So, I called him the great snake.

Some Sundays we would catch the train to Margate and go to Dreamland an amusement centre, popular with young people. Afterwards we'd catch the train back to Tunbridge Wells.

The great snake was fond of salads, so we would have tea in the café above the Ritz Cinema, then go to the evening film. Cinema performances were continuous, and you could go in at any time. There would be a B picture followed by a Pathé newsreel then the feature film.

The usherettes would show you to your seat with their torches, and in the intervals, they would come around with refreshments. They carried a large tray in front of them held by a leather strap around their neck. This tray had ice creams, sweets, chocolate and I think cigarettes. They had a large leather purse and they would take the money and give you any change. Sometimes these sales would go on when the next picture had started, so they were carried on by torchlight. Some cinemas had an organ that would rise up out of the pit in front of the screen and the organist would play away during the interval.

Reginald Dixon was a famous organist at the time, who played mainly in Blackpool. I'm not sure if he came to our local cinema, but there were others who did.

**

Tonbridge sports ground had facilities for tennis, bowls, and a putting green. We would have a go on the putting green and try to chat up any girls and to generally show off. The green keeper was a belligerent old devil. In addition to the green fee, you had to leave a deposit of half a crown with him, for the hire of the putters and the ball. When these were taken back, he would always try to argue that the ball had been damaged and refuse to give you the deposit back. We would not leave without it, and if any girls were having the same trouble, we would argue for them. This sometimes led to a date.

Barden Road ran alongside the river and there was a boat house and a landing stage where canoes could be hired. This was another popular venue for the young. We would hire a canoe and paddle around looking to see what girls we could impress. Sometimes this led to harmless fun when we would splash each other when passing. If the boat keeper saw this, he would call us in.

In summer after work we would go swimming at the locks, farther down the Medway. This became popular with other young lads and gals, and at weekends we would often all gather for a picnic. We would have fun diving off the riverbank to see who could get to the other side quickest. This often resulted in a competition between the boys trying to impress the girls.

If you were lucky you could get one of the girls to go to the pictures with you. Going to the pictures meant getting a seat in the back row that you hoped would lead to a 'snogging' session. The young, back then, did not have the sexual freedom that prevails today. If you got as far as getting your hand on her suspenders, you'd had a good night.

The Castle Hotel, next to the High Street river bridge, had become our regular pub. The landlady was a widow who ran it with her daughter. I was secretary of the Christmas Club and I would sit in the public bar on Friday nights from seven p.m. to eight p.m. where I would take the money from the customers.

Those who knew me, did not let on that I was underage. They would give me what they wanted to save towards Christmas, and I would enter it into the book. Then I'd total it up and hand it over to the landlady. Some weeks when they were hard up, they'd have a 'sub' off the book. There was a dartboard there and Dad and I played, together with several others, including Percy Pankhurst who lived next door to us. He was home after serving most of the war as a POW in Germany and was working in the loco sheds.

The other players were Arthur Gurr, who had a boot and shoe repair shop in The Botany, Arthur Sharp and Harry Critenden from the top end of the town and three others who made up the team. Jack Lucas and Jimmy Courvain who'd served in the navy and Tommy Mundy who'd been in the army. They were all happy go lucky characters and they could consume large quantities of beer.

These three always fancied themselves as what was known then as a lady's man. Tommy would dress in a dark suit with a collar and tie and he always carried a comb in his top pocket. He would often take it out and dip it into his beer, and he would then comb his hair.

We formed a team and we played in the Tonbridge Darts League. I was also the scorer and I chalked up the score totals on the blackboard. The leading team was from 'The Gallopers' further down Tonbridge High Street. Their star player was Hector Russell. He was a bumptious little man and Dad hated him. When our team met them, there was always intense rivalry. Jim Pike was the News of the World Darts Champion and he came to Tonbridge to give an exhibition. Hector Russell played him and lost, much to Dad's delight.

Some Sunday lunchtimes when the pubs turned out, Jack, Jimmy and Tommy would take some pies and sandwiches and go down to the boathouse where I'd learned to swim. I would go with them and we'd spend the afternoon there. Jack Lucas had long wavy hair and he would dive in and then just lie there on the surface for a long time, as though he'd passed out. Just as we were about to dive in to help him, he would lift his head and swim to the other side.

They would stay there till the effects of the beer had worn off, and then they would go back to the pub when it opened. I would go home, and then Dad and I would join them again in the evening.

When Dusty was 'home' he would join us. He arranged a match in Cranbrook and Gran put us up for the weekend. One of the pubs in Cranbrook had selected a team and put up a challenge with money at stake. I do not remember the amount, but we won and there was much celebrating.

About this time Gran and Dusty moved back to Tonbridge. Gran's sister Fan had married George Pilbeam who had a smallholding in Higham Lane. Dusty bought a caravan, and they lived on the smallholding and put their name on the Council housing waiting list.

In the winter despite all their efforts, they could not prevent condensation, and this made it uncomfortable. They lived like that for some time before they eventually got a small council flat at the top end of the town.

***

I saw a photo of Reg Park who had won the Mr Britain contest, and it encouraged me to begin weight training to develop my physique. I bought a set of weights and I began training in my bedroom. The barbell weighed 90lbs. I remember that when it was delivered everyone struggled when they tried to lift it. To their amazement I was able to lift it straight above my head. The Health and Strength magazine published training routines and I followed these for my workouts.

By the time I became eligible for call-up I was in very good physical shape. Conscription had continued after the war, and young men were called up to serve two years in the armed forces. I applied to join the Royal Marines, and on reaching eighteen, I was requested to go to the marine barracks in Chatham for a test. I passed and I was told that I would be sent for in due course. I was delighted and I went off to celebrate with another lad.

The Chatham Empire Theatre had a variety show and we went to the matinee performance. Halfway through, a plump middle-aged woman dressed in a tutu and carrying a magic wand came on. She started singing 'nobody loves a fairy when she's forty'. All the sailors in the audience started booing and barracking her.

A big marine sergeant in the front row stood up and shouted, "Why don't you lot shut up and give the poor old cow a chance!" Everything went quiet.

She walked to the edge of the stage and said, "Thank you, young man, I'm glad to see that there's at least one gentleman in the audience."

My delight at having passed was short lived. With the war over, the government decided to cut the number of armed forces and so recruiting to the Marines was halted. I had a letter informing me of this and instructing me to report to the Royal West Kent barracks in Maidstone.

Army life presented no problems to me, coming from my background, and I revelled in the life. I enjoyed the drilling and the physical activities, and I completed eight weeks of basic training. You then undertook the Basic Infantry test. I still have the result and they are as follows:

HJ (high jump) 7, LJ (long jump) 10, KB 10, EB 10, 1 mile 10, 5 miles 10, Total points 67, Total percent 95.7.

Before being posted, I was interviewed by the Personnel Selection Officer who asked me what my choice was. Having been disappointed at not becoming a marine, I told him that the infantry would do. He said that he thought that I could do better than that and he sent me for a mechanics exam. This is what I always describe as 'The Fickle Finger of Fate' as it was to change the whole course of my life. It was 1947 and I was eighteen years old.

I had little difficulty with the questions as I had always tinkered about with my motorbike. He told me that I'd done better than many who were apprentices, and so he was sending me to Wales on a driver mechanics course.

After a week's leave I reported to Kinmel Park Camp, Rhyl. This was an eight-week course of hands on mechanics, book learning about the theory, and driving instruction. There was a gymnasium there where I continued to train.

Sometimes in our barrack room I'd organise a game where we would run down the room and dive over the table onto a mattress. For those who could do this, chairs were then added to the other side until such time as you couldn't clear them. In order to increase the distance that you could dive, I would fetch the springboard from the gym.

One weekend they held the Army versus the RAF Boxing Championships. We had to provide the supporting bouts. These took the form of 'milling' contests. You went into the ring with an opponent, where you would proceed to knock the shit out of each other for one minute. Each team lined up at opposite sides of the ring, and you were given either a red or a green singlet to identify which team you were in. Each side would have matching weight categories so as to make the contest level. Unfortunately, there weren't enough singlets to go around, and so you had to quickly get one from a guy who came out of the ring.

When my first time came, I hadn't been given a singlet, so the next guy went in. I was a cruiser weight (light heavyweight) and having missed my turn I was sent in against the heavyweight. His name was Bill Steel and he was much taller than me and he outreached me. He kept hitting me in the face as I tried to get near him, and it frustrated me.

Next time around I made sure that I went in the right weight division, and this time it was 'Tich' Ward. He was a tough little guy, but I had the reach advantage. I punched him all around the ring and I took my frustration out on him. Despite this, we all remained good friends afterwards. I was surprised to learn recently that milling contests are still practised as part of the training for the special forces.

At the end of the course I passed my driving test at Conwy, driving a Q6 Bedford lorry. I also came joint second in the final exam with ninety-six percent, with Pete Gower, who had been a mechanic by trade.

I was then sent to Newbury on another course and I spent six weeks in a factory working on petrol engines. When the course finished, I was given a stripe and a driver/mechanics badge for my tunic. I was then posted to Salisbury as Lance Bombardier Saunders, to join the 23rd Field Regiment RA.

I was put in charge of the vehicles of E (Eagle) troop. There was a Bedford Q lorry, a Chrysler armoured car, a Bren Gun carrier, a 15 cwt Pick Up and a Quad. My job was to maintain them with regular servicing and to deal with any minor breakdowns. Anything needing major repairs was carried out by the battery workshop.

I also drove the Quad, towing a 25-pounder gun and limber, together with the gunnery sergeant and four gunners, and we went on training exercises on Salisbury Plain.

Every Wednesday, I would drive them to Churchill's old college in Marlborough to give their boy cadets gunnery training.

At lunchtimes the gunners would all go to the school canteen for a meal. The cadet sergeant major would take my sergeant and me to lunch. I would drive us into the town to a little bakery shop that had a restaurant above. This had tables and chairs with white linen tablecloths and proper linen serviettes. There were silver knives and forks and the waitresses wore little frilly pinnies and bonnets. This was another eye opener for me, and I enjoyed the new experience.

I had been put on the duty rostrum when I first arrived, which meant that I had to do guard duty. While patrolling at night I could never keep awake during the early hours.

One night while doing the two a.m. till four a.m. patrol, I went down to the garages and I climbed into the cab of a lorry parked on the parade ground. I went off to sleep and I was awakened by voices. It was early dawn and standing right in front of the cab below me, were the guard sergeant and the duty officer. Luckily, they never looked up to see me. I waited until it was all clear and then I went back to the guard room.

When they asked where I'd been all night, I kicked up a fuss and said that I'd been walking about, waiting for my relief. I think that they had their doubts, but I got away with it.

After that, I made sure that I was given the job as driver to the duty officer. I wangled it, as the regular officer had a motorbike that I used to maintain for him. Then on guard nights, I was only required to drive the officer to the Larkhill Camp and back, and then I could kip down in the guardhouse for the rest of the night.

My opposite number was Hughie (Nobby) Clarke, the D/M of F Troop, and we soon became 'muckers'. Nobby was a scouser from Liverpool and we had lots in common.

One weekend we got a travel pass and he came home with me to Tonbridge. This was in order to bring my set of weights back to the camp. I had persuaded the NCO in charge of the camp cinema to let me keep them in the projection room. When we carried them along the station platform, with one end of the barbell on each of our shoulders, with the weights in the middle, the other passengers looked mystified.

Nobby wasn't interested in weightlifting, and so I used to train alone. Soon our C.O. Major Hogg got to hear of it and one day he sent for me. He had orders to improve the men's fitness and HQ were sending four instructors from the Army Physical Training Corps to do this. He told me that I was being attached to them to help.

We undertook training sessions with teams doing running, gymnastic exercises, boxing and general physical training. This lasted for several weeks until it was considered that the squaddies were fit enough.

After this there was an inspection and a display demonstration on the parade ground. General William 'Bill' Slim came down to review it, together with other big wigs. The four instructors and I were selected to do a demonstration in front of them.

Dressed in full battle gear and carrying a rifle, we had to pick up another soldier, sling him over our shoulders and run across the parade ground to the other side. I do not know how it got there, but a piece of brick lay on the tarmac in front of me as I started running across. I saw it too late and I tripped over it. I went sprawling and I shot the soldier off onto the ground. I scrambled up, picked up my rifle and slung the soldier back over my shoulders and completed the course. I expected to be put on a charge in front of Major Hogg the next morning, but instead of that he commended me for showing fortitude by finishing.

***

On my days off, I would catch the bus to Devizes. At the swimming pool, a towel and trunks could be hired, and I'd spend the afternoon swimming.

One day I noticed a girl sunbathing who took my fancy. She had long blonde hair and a figure like Ester Williams. I chatted her up and I took her to the pictures that evening. After that I met her regularly and I even went home with her and met her parents. She was mad keen on dogs and she had applied for a job as a kennel girl at a Greyhound Stadium. Shortly after that she went to London and I never saw her again.

A group of us from our battery were sent to Didcot to join a group of Land Girls, who needed help in picking up potatoes from the farm fields. We were put under canvas with six of us to a tent. We slept on the ground with our feet towards the centre pole.

The latrines were in a long wooden shed. This had a large sewage pipe that came up out of the ground at one end, ran across the ground and disappeared back into the ground at the other end. Spaced along it were partitions made of sacking and each partition had a section of the pipe that had a round hole cut in it. Water continually ran through the pipe and you had to squat over it when needed.

Nobby and I thought that we'd have some fun, so we bought some little candles and fitted them onto pieces of wood. One morning, when all the partitions were occupied, we went up to the end with the candles. We then lit them and floated them on the water running through the pipe. We had a good laugh hearing the cries and swearing that followed.

Nobby became friendly with one of the Land Girls and I did not see much of him after that. After we got back to the regiment, he received a letter and he was worried for a while. He told me later that it was from the land girl who thought that she was pregnant, but it turned out to be a false alarm.

***

Eagle troop and F troop from our battery were chosen to take part in a tattoo at Southsea Castle. It lasted for two weeks, and twice a day our gunners would give a demonstration and fire off blanks. Nobby and I would drive on with our team of gunners, they would unhitch the gun and limber, and we'd drive off. When they'd finished, we would drive back, and after they had been hitched up, drive them off again.

The evening performance ended at nine p.m. and after that Nobby and I would go off down to the seafront that was nearby. We met a couple of girls from Bath who were there on holiday.

After the tattoo had finished, we used to write to them from our camp in Tilshead. We arranged for them to meet us halfway. They took the train and we would join them. We 'borrowed' the officer's motorbike for this until he found out and put a stop to it. There was no other way of getting there by public transport, so we had to resort to using a couple of old bicycles to bike each way. This soon proved too exhausting and we decided that the effort wasn't worth it.

A young gunner named Jessop was given special leave to attend his sister's wedding. There was also a regular who was due to be demobbed. Nobby was ordered to drive them to Salisbury station in his Quad.

Shortly after they left, we had a message to say there had been an accident on Salisbury Plain.

I drove an officer and two others to the scene and when we got there the Quad was overturned on its side. Nobby and the regular were unharmed, but Jessop was trapped underneath. I remember seeing him and his face had turned black. I think that he was killed instantly.

There was an inquiry and Nobby was exonerated. I think that he was lucky as the Quad had overturned on a bend. He could have been driving too fast, but I never said anything. A detachment from the regiment, including Nobby, attended the funeral in Liverpool.

I played football for the battery and our regimental goalkeeper was named Blowers. He was a regular soldier and shortly afterwards he ended his service.

When I got leave, Dad and I would go and watch Arsenal, who he supported. I remember seeing Leslie Compton who played centre half, and his brother Denis Compton, the famous cricketer, play on the wing.

Tonbridge also had a football team who were in the Southern League. They played on The Angel ground in Vale Road. On leave again, I went to see them play, and to my surprise who should be their goalkeeper but George Blowers. At the end of the match I took Dad to the dressing room and I introduced him.

***

In the run up to the Korean War our regiment was sent to Singapore to form up with the 27th Brigade Group. Nobby and I were billeted in Grays, Essex, and we were given the job of ferrying all the vehicles onto the waiting ships. There were also some little Hillman cars that were being exported to Bulawayo, which was then in Southern Rhodesia. I got to drive one and I had never experienced a gear lever fitted to the steering wheel before.

The dockers union ran the docks as a 'closed shop' and the dockers were not happy in their attitude towards us. They objected to us being allowed to load the ships, but they could not do anything about it. At lunchtime, they would all down tools and sit on the barges all afternoon playing cards. I had never seen the like of so much money changing hands every day.

We were there for two weeks, and as we both had less than six months left to serve, it wasn't worth us being sent back

to our regiment. Nobby was posted somewhere up north and I was sent to Camberley to join the Brigade of Guards. We never saw each other again and we lost touch.

***

I joined Kings Troop Fourth RHA (Royal Horse Artillery) but my unit did not have horses. We had SPs (self-propelled guns). These were Sherman tanks with their turrets removed and replaced with 25 pounder guns, protected by thick armoured plating.

The officer was Major Hoare who interviewed me. I'd never worked with tanks before. The only tracked vehicle that I'd worked with was a Bren Gun carrier. The sergeant in charge of running the MT store (Mechanical Transport) had recently retired, so the major decided that I would be a suitable replacement.

I soon settled in, I did not report to the duty office and I kept my head down. This meant that I would avoid parades and any guard duties unless they found out. Fortunately, they never did. I fixed up a camp bed at the back of the store and I only went to the main barracks for meals.

My job in the store was to issue spares and equipment to anyone who presented a requisition note.

Major Hoare was fond of the ladies and he had quite a few acquaintances. He had a dark green HRG 1500, open top sports car. It had twin carburettors that were in constant need of tuning. I kept it running sweetly for him, and after lunch he would be off for the rest of the day. I'd then close the store and spend the afternoon in the NAAFI playing billiards or table tennis.

There was a café nearby that made delicious ham sandwiches. The girl there would be at the counter making them. She was very attractive, and she wore a close-fitting jumper that emphasized her ample proportions. She would clutch the loaf to her body and cut each slice in an upward movement. I winced at the thought of what might happen if the knife slipped.

My time in the army expired and I was released on 14 December, 1949. Major Hoare interviewed me before I left and he offered to promote me to sergeant if I signed on for another three years. I thought about it but I decided to return to civvy street.

He wrote the following testimonial in my Soldiers Release Book: 'L/Bdr. Saunders has been employed as a driver and as an MT clerk. He is a clean, smart NCO with a thorough knowledge of MT maintenance, accounting and procedure. He is very conscientious, well mannered, trustworthy and reliable. A very good young NCO.'

I REST MY CASE.

Chapter 8

My actual demob took place at Aldershot where I received two weeks paid leave and a demob suit.

I returned to live with Mum and Dad and the domestic situation was placid, but Mum was still having bouts of depression. I hadn't decided what I'd do, and I decided to take a couple of weeks before looking for a job.

I happened to meet Eileen, who was still working as an usherette. I asked her out and we dated a few times. Taking her home one night she asked me what I intended doing.

I remember that I showed her my hands and I said, "I've only got these."

There was nothing serious between us and one night we went to 'The Bull' public house in the High Street. During the evening I saw a young ATS girl who was home on leave. She took my fancy and we got talking. At turn out time I asked if I could take her home to Tunbridge Wells. Luckily 'the great snake' (Alec Mitchell) was also in the bar, so I got him to take Eileen home and I went off with the other girl. I never saw Eileen after that, and I never saw the ATS girl again either.

***

I decided not to go back to building work and plumbing, and instead I'd try for a job back on the railway, in the Signal and Telegraph Department, where I'd been as a boy.

The old inspector had retired, and it was now a little guy named Holden running the show. The sub inspector was also new. Norman Pearson 'Pidge' was still the Chief Linesman. They took me on, and I was given various jobs.

At first, I went around with the Tonbridge Linesman Bob Bartholomew and his assistant Harry Ralph. Bob knew all there was to know about railway signalling and telephones. He was an excellent teacher and I quickly learned to install and maintain the equipment.

I worked with him and Harry, in the signal boxes and on the tracks. Signalling then was a lot different than now, but the principle is much the same. The old-time signal boxes had heavy levers that the signalman pulled to operate the signals. These were semaphore signals on gantries, that were moved up and down by wires and pulleys that ran along beside the track. Points, that shifted the rails to divert a train onto another line, were also operated by levers. These points were shifted by a series of metal rods that also ran from the signal box. However, the signalman could not just operate them at will, as there was a 'locking' system.

Behind the row of levers, there was an illuminated map of all the lines on each side of the signal box. This had 'eyeballs' that would indicate where any train was. When a train entered a section, the eyeball would flip to red and the levers would be locked.

Out on the track the rails were bonded together into different sections, and a DC current was fed through them. This energised a relay in the signal box. When the train entered each section, its wheels and axles shorted out the current, and this caused the relay to drop, thus locking the levers, and the 'eyeball' would flip to red. This safety system prevented two trains from being allowed into the same section. The Mechanical Linesman, Arthur Shoebridge and his assistant Bill Weekes, were responsible for the mechanical side, and we dealt with the electrical part.

Out along the track there were battery cupboards that provided the DC current. The batteries were made up from small round sacks from which a carbon stick protruded. This had a zinc rod connected to it, and they were immersed in jars filled with water and crystals. If the zinc rod dissolved, it broke the circuit and the signal box could not function. Before this happened all of it had to be renewed.

Harry and I carried them along the track, which was hard work walking along the sleepers. Doing this to the 'distant' signals was very tiring. I soon used my motorbike for this, using the country lanes to get me close to the signals.

At the junctions where the points were, the circuits ran through metal boxes in the middle of the track. There were connecting rods to each rail and when the points were operated, this switched the contacts inside the box. Each box was screwed to a sleeper and the hinged lid fastened down with bolts. Working on them was dangerous, as you had to keep an eye out for any approaching trains.

It was also somewhat unhygienic. Carriages then had toilets that emptied directly onto the track. Passing trains would leave effluent and used toilet paper, splattered all over the boxes. This had to be cleaned off before they could be opened. We had no protective clothing and I wonder what Health and Safety would say now?

In winter, the boxes produced condensation which would drip onto the contacts inside. This doesn't matter as water is a conductor. But in sub-zero temperatures, this freezes and breaks the circuit, as ice is an insulator. We would often be called out to deal with this in bad weather.

The telephone side was much easier, and Bob taught me the circuitry so that I could deal with any telephone faults. At times there would be a line fault, which meant going up the poles. Instead of carrying a ladder all along the track we used 'leg irons'. These were not like you see today. Ours were just a metal rod that strapped to your leg, with a spur at the bottom. To climb the pole, these spurs had to be dug in each side, and you worked your way up grasping the pole.

Nearing the top one day, one spur hit a knot and I slipped back down the pole collecting two hands full of splinters. A common fault was a 'dry' joint, where the cable connected to the wires. This had to be cleaned and then soldered. The soldering iron had a metal cup on the end that held a small round cartridge. Climbing up the pole with them, and perching there, wasn't easy. You then thrust a lighted match into the cartridge, which caused it to burn fiercely, producing a terrific heat. The new joint could then be soldered. On windy days you had to make sure that you weren't facing into the wind, or it would blow back on you.

Our telephone exchange and switchboard were situated next to the parcel office and the police office. Josie, one of the operators, would sit there with her skirt above her knees. When she was on duty and I went to fix a fault, I would quite often find detective Huggett there. Also, when Bob went missing, it was a good bet that you'd find him there. I didn't like her, as she was too 'loud' for my taste.

We also had instruments that were operated with liquid mercury. Bob would dismantle them on the bench if they had a fault. The mercury would run out over the bench in volatile globules. We would cup our hands and chase them around, guiding them into a jar. Today this would probably be regarded as a health hazard.

When the Permanent Way renewed the track, this was carried out on Saturday nights and Sunday mornings, so as not to disrupt the service. We had to be there to re-bond the new rails. The rails were connected with 'plates' that were bolted through each rail. We had to fit spacing pieces between them, to insulate our circuits. The other rails had to be bonded, to ensure that the current passed through them to complete the circuit. This was done by drilling the rail each side and inserting a copper rod. For drilling the rails, we had a machine fitted with a chain and sprocket.

After clamping it to the rail you bent over it and turned the handle, tightening the drill as you went. Drills soon became blunted, and after several hours of this, your arms would be aching. Signal box work was mostly carried out on Sundays. All this work was additional to the working week but was welcomed because of the pay structure. Saturday nights were time and a half, and Sunday's double time.

If I wasn't working, on Sundays I would go swimming. Tonbridge had an unheated open-air pool that attracted lots of young people. I met up with Den Sumbling and Derek 'Deg' Fields. We would often perform handstands and feats of strength on the grass lawn by the pool. Later we were joined by Ian Russell a brawny chap who liked to wrestle.

Den's married brother was living in the top flat of an old Victorian house, that had a basement with its own entrance. This basement was unoccupied, so I suggested that we rent it and use it for a gym. I contacted the landlord and I rented it for ten shillings (50p) a week. We were given some old mattresses, and Deg acquired a set of parallel bars. I provided the weights and some other items of equipment. We would train and work out there several evenings a week. Ian liked to box, and we also practised Judo. Deg and I also liked to perform handstand feats.

At the time there was a variety act in the West End called 'Les Trios des Milles'. This was strong man Rueb Martin, Rusty Sellers and Len Talbot. Their act was a brilliant combination of various handstands and balancing, performed to the music of Rossini's 'The Thieving Magpie'. Deg and I started our own routine and we would often show off down at the pool.

There were two vacancies in our department, and Den and Deg applied and they started as installers in one of the gangs.

Deg saw a Triumph car advertised and I took him to buy it. It was a very old 1930s Standard Eight. He drove it home and I followed on my motorbike. We hadn't gone far when he suddenly came to a stop, and as I drew alongside, he waved the gear lever out of the window. It had snapped off at the base and so he could not change gear. I took him to a garage, and they were able to weld it back on. I wondered if the seller had known that it was dodgy.

Working for the railway meant that you were entitled to privileged travel, and one free pass a year. Deg and I saw an advert for a week's holiday in Jersey. It was a holiday camp at St. Brelade's Bay. We got tickets to Portsmouth and caught the afternoon ferry. There were crowds of people getting on, and it struck me how shabbily dressed they were. It reminded me of the pictures of refugees during the war. I had a brand-new trench coat that had been made for me at Burtons.

The only space available was standing along the decks, with our suitcases at our feet. Soon after we sailed the crew members came around and fitted tarpaulins to the handrails and roped them to the deck above. It wasn't long before I realised why. It was to be the roughest crossing ever known.

The waves battered the ferry and the decks were awash. Everyone was seasick and the luggage came floating along the deck together with vomit. I saw one lot with a chicken wishbone in it and I was left wondering who could have brought that up. I went aft and I wedged myself between the stern and the flagpole.

One minute I could touch the sea and next it was thirty feet below me. The crossing took sixteen hours, and when daylight came, I could see our sister ship, the Empress of Guernsey, on our starboard side. The bow was ploughing down into the waves, and as it came up it was throwing the water back over the funnel. My trench coat had turned white from the salt spray.

When we landed in St Helier, I could see that our ship's side that was covered with vomit. We caught the bus to the holiday camp and clapped out in our chalet.

We soon recovered and we began to enjoy camp life.

One night in the bar we met two girls. In conversation I mentioned that I had a motorbike and that Deg had a car. When he told them, that his car was a Triumph they were impressed. Triumphs at that time were very sporty models, but he failed to mention that his was a 1930s old banger. Later, we took them back to their chalets. Mine was sharing with her mother, so I said goodnight and I went back to our chalet. Deg did not come back till morning.

The camp entertainer was a young comedian, singer and dancer. He was very good, and I think that it was Bruce Forsyth at the beginning of his career. Every Friday night they held a talent contest where campers were encouraged to take part. Deg and I had put a balancing routine together, and we would practice at the pool, and on the lawn in front of the chalets. Some of the campers thought that we were a professional act. When we said that we were only amateurs, they said that we should enter the competition.

We intended to but we saw a flight to France advertised that only went on Fridays. I had neither flown nor been to France, so that won out. The plane was a De Havilland Q6 Rapide. It was a twin engine bi-plane capable of carrying six passengers. We sat behind the pilot who was dressed in sports jacket and trousers. I remember looking down and seeing large shoals of silver fish in the sea. We landed at St Malo and we spent the day in Dinard. I thought that going to a Café in mid-afternoon and buying a cognac was quite something. We even tried some snails in garlic, but I thought that they tasted like rubber grommets.

***

I continued to work out at our gym, for two to three hours nightly. We all used weights and I also practised Judo. Ian liked to get the gloves on and spar with me. The muscle magazines were full of pictures of bodybuilders with astonishingly muscular physiques. They advertised Joe Weider's anabolic steroids that were used to build muscle size. I never used them, as I thought that their long-term effects could be harmful. In any case my motivation was to build strength for gymnastic purposes and not just for muscle size.

The tenants in the flat above the gym would ask us up to watch boxing, when it was on the BBC. They had a little black and white television set with a six-inch screen. I remember watching the amateur lightweight Dick McTaggart in his early days.

The Southern Railway in Tonbridge had a boxing team, and a featherweight named Lock would come and train with us. Bob Bartholomew's youngest son Ray was keen to compete, and Bob asked me if he could come and train with us. I agreed and he trained with us and we sparred with him.

On the night of his son's first fight, Bob asked me to go with him to watch. Mr and Mrs Warnett and their daughters, who used to live above us in Vale Road, now lived in Tonbridge High Street. I knew that Bob often called in on them on his way to work. He turned up at the fight and he brought their daughter Jill with him. I could not remember her from when they had lived near us. She was sixteen, and in her final year at the County School. She enjoyed sports, she was a member of the Tonbridge Athletic Club and she also played in a table tennis team.

Ray lost his fight and he lost interest in training. I thought no more about it.

Soon after that, Bob would arrive at work with cakes and pastries that Jill had baked for me. She was a good cook, having been taught by her mother. This continued for some time, then Bob suggested that I repay her by taking her to the pictures. I agreed, but when we met, I told her that it would be strictly platonic, as my time and interest was taken up by my training.

Jill left school and she went to work as a clerk for Wisden, the cricket ball makers. She caught the train to Hidenborough every morning, and I would often see her, and after a while we began to date.

***

At about this time, Australia was advertising for young men to work in their mica mines. It was good pay, and it was said that after a year you could return home with a thousand pounds. That was attractive to Deg and I, and he went to Australia House in London for the papers. Before we'd made up our minds, he was upgraded to a post in Southampton, and my mother's health was not good, so we did not go.

I continued to work with Bob. One day the inspector sent for me to say that he wanted me to take over the stores. The storeman then was Harold Austin and he was away sick. That came easy to me and it meant that I could also train in the store during the day. The ladders were hung on brackets from the roof, and I would use them to perform hand over hand exercises and repetition back planches. I would often entertain the men with feats of balancing and flips, on the work benches.

Our depot also had a lorry, and I would drive it to Wimbledon every week to pick up materials from the main stores. I would also drive 'Pidge' and the inspector to a pub in Sussex. Food rationing was still in force and there was a black market in sugar. The landlord in the pub sold sugar, and he also kept pigs that he slaughtered and sold. This was illegal at the time. My job was to make sure that Detective Huggett and his sidekick did not get wind of it, as they had a car. We knew that he was suspicious, but I managed to outwit him.

Sometimes, Inspector Holden would get me to drive him down to a pub in Heathfield. I would drop him off, and he would tell me to pick him up at four-thirty p.m. I'd then go on to our Eastbourne depot.

After lunch, I would drive to Pevensey Beach and spend the afternoon swimming and sunbathing and I would then go back and pick him up. He would be so drunk that he could hardly stand. I'd get him into the cab and then drive him to his flat in Catford. By the time I got back to the depot everyone had gone. I made sure that I booked two hours overtime and it was never queried. Sometime later, when I'd left the railway, I heard that he'd been imprisoned for embezzlement.

My time in the store ended several months later, when Harold returned to work. I then joined Charlie Payne our Sevenoaks Linesman, as his assistant. Charlie was an amiable chap, and at lunchtimes we would sit in the hut and play cards for a few pence. He liked to play Cribbage but he was a bad loser. He always considered me lucky and he would often throw the cards out of the window in frustration. We got on well, however, and we became good friends.

By this time, I was going steady with Jill, and sometimes we would go to Charlie's house for dinner. His wife, Eve, was a good cook and Jill and Eve became friends. We'd all play cards in the evening and Charlie was mostly able to control his outbursts.

The railway embankments close to our hut were infested with rabbits. Charlie had a ferret that he kept there, and we would go rabbiting. We would fix nets over the rabbit holes and then put the ferret down, further along the bank. Pretty soon, the rabbits would come flying out of the holes. Some would run out from holes that we had not covered, but quite a few would get caught in the nets. It was then a rush to get to them and poleaxe them before they could escape.

Charlie would sell those that he did not want, to a butcher for a few shillings. Neither Charlie nor I was in the Union. I was against them, on the premise that I had always fended for myself, and I did not want a Union telling me what to do. The Union called a strike in Tonbridge but Charlie and I ignored it and we went to work as normal. When we walked through the picket lines, they booed us and called us blacklegs. They 'sent us to Coventry'
but we did not care. Later they called it off and I cannot remember what it was about.

***

I sold my Triumph Speed Twin and I bought a new 650cc Thunderbird. Jill enjoyed the thrill of pillion riding. Sometimes I would take my hands off the handlebars and hold my arms out like wings. Using just my hips to steer, I would then weave in and out of the broken white lines. Other times, I would open it up, and I would then bend down over the handlebars, so that she caught the full force of the slipstream. Neither of us wore helmets or any form of protective clothing and we loved the feeling of pure freedom. Her parents did not know, as they would probably have had a fit.

Jill's cousin, Jack Neal, was living with them. He'd left the Tarmac company, where he'd been driving the steam roller, and he was working for Woodman's, the Ironmongers shop in High Street. He repaired customers' lawn mowers and he cut keys. Jack could repair practically

101

everything, and he enjoyed tinkering with anything mechanical. He had an OHC Velocette which continually broke down. He kept it in the outhouse next to their living room and he would be working on the engine most nights.

Sometimes I would not leave Jill's house till after midnight, and Jack would still be working on an engine. When he'd reassembled the engine, he would be anxious to know if he'd cured the leak. He was reluctant to start it up at that time of night, but I used to convince him that it would not disturb anyone. The sound must have woken up most of the High Street.

Jack had a great sense of humour and we became lifelong friends. Jill's father, Len, was also easy-going and he did not mind much what Jack got up to. One time though, Jack had taken one of his Aunt's backing trays and had left it full of oil on the floor, with a chain soaking in it. Len went to fetch something, and he stepped into it. He was angry at the time, but afterwards we all saw the funny side of it.

I remember one night we were all playing table tennis on their kitchen table. We would hit the ball then run around the table, and the next one would hit it back, and so on. There weren't enough bats to go around, so Jack used one of his aunt's dinner plates. Rushing to hit the ball he hit the plate against the edge of the table, and it broke into little pieces.

Never at a loss for an answer, he said, "Well Auntie, it was cracked."

Sometimes we'd go off to places like Stonehenge, Blackbushe Airport, or Camber Sands for the day. Jack had made two pannier boxes for his Velocette, and with Jean, his future wife, we four would take a picnic with us. The Velocette had no rear springing and the tomatoes were always squashed. Some evenings we'd all go down to Hastings for a fish and chip supper at Jill's Grill.

With another couple, Ken and Joyce Eaton, we'd spend a day on Eastbourne beach. Ken had made a Jokari game with two wooden bats. We would mark out a court in the sand and spend hours hitting the ball back and forth. When the tide was in, we would swim out to a large iron marker, hang onto it to rest, and then swim back. It wasn't until years later that we found out that it was the marker to where the untreated effluent from the town was discharged.

The depot's electrician was Charlie Oughton, who had a Triumph Tiger 100. If I'd been working Saturday night, I'd grab a little sleep and I was then free to go out on Sunday.

Charlie, Jill and I, would go to Brands Hatch when there was motor racing there. They were 500cc racing cars and it was very exciting. The track was much smaller than it is now and sitting on the bank beside the clubhouse you could see around the whole circuit. Unlike today, success was all down to the driver's skill. I think that Formula One today is boring.

In a recent radio interview with a leading technician, with many years' experience designing modern racing cars, when asked what part the driver now played, she replied ten percent. With the 500cc cars there was much overtaking and dicing on the corners.

Although sometimes accidents happened, I only witnessed one fatality. At the end of the afternoon they staged a mechanics race. I saw a car go off the track and through a fence. It seemed simple enough, but the mechanic was killed.

Drivers like Stirling Moss in the Cooper, and Jim Clarke and Graham Hill, all raced there, as did John Surtees. Jill's favourite was Paul Emery who drove the Emeryson. There were also amateur drivers like George Wickens who owned a dairy in Maidstone.

A magazine seller would come around calling out, "Get your Autocar magazine — LE MANS edition."

The race commentary would come over the tannoy. This was given by John Bolster. He was a great character with a handlebar moustache, and he reminded me of Jimmy Edwards. He was also a racing driver and he had built his own hill climber that he ran on Methanol. He said that the engine enjoyed its alcohol as much as its owner. Charlie Oughton died shortly afterwards at the age of thirty-four from kidney failure.

***

One day I was called and I was told that Head Office had said that all new signals and gantries, were to be made at our Tonbridge Depot. The

Inspector told me that I was being sent to Ashford on a two-week course, with another guy named Ron Town. We were to learn acetylene cutting and welding and we would then be given the job of making the signals. This was another example of 'The Fickle Finger of Fate', for it was to change the whole direction of my life.

I enjoyed the course, and when we'd finished it, we began cutting up old rails and drilling them for the new signals. I would take the lorry up to Wimbledon and bring back the fittings. We assembled them on the ground, and they were then stripped down and taken to the site. One of the gangs would erect them, Ron and I would then re-assemble them. Whilst I was cutting the sheet steel, I also cut out some large circles and I welded them together. I then drilled a hole through the middle that fitted our barbell and took them to our gym. I also made a pulley machine and incline bench to add to our training equipment.

Jack Neal was also a keen photographer. He married and they rented a flat above a greengrocer in Tonbridge High Street. His wife Jean was pleased, because she said that she would never need to buy vegetables.

They shared a bathroom with a couple who lived in the flat above them. It was on the landing and Jack used it as a dark room. When Iris Hart came down for a bath, she would have to move Jack's negatives that were strung above it. She also complained that his developer had turned the bath black.

Mum made me some posing trunks and Jack took some physique photos of me. I sent them to the Health and Strength Magazine, and they were published. This encouraged me to do some more and I entered a photo for the 'Bodybuilder of the Month' competition. It won and it was published with an article about my training methods. The prize was a session in the London studio of John Graham. He was the official photographer for the Mr Universe contest.

Mum made me a better pair of trunks, and off I went. He took some photos and shortly afterwards I appeared on the cover of the Muscle Magazine 'Vigour'. I did not receive any payment but I could always say that I'd been a 'Cover Man'.

I continued working with Ron, and one day I found out that he was a 'runner' for Bob Bert the Bookie. I would see him collect the bets, and quite often there were winners, but at the end of the week the bookie always seemed to finish in front.

Ron was getting a shilling in the pound commission, and I offered him one and sixpence if he handed the smaller bets to me. I soon got the hang of it and I learned how to work out the various combinations. I had no difficulty in calculating the odds, and pretty soon I was making as much money doing that, as I was getting as wages.

The Sub Inspector got to hear of it, and he told me to stop or he would see to it that I got the sack. I had never liked him, so I told him he could keep the job and I left.

Mum agreed that I could use our front room as an office, and I had a telephone installed. I began going around the railway depots each morning and collecting bets. The local bookies would only pay out winners at very restricted odds and they had very low limits on what you could win.

I offered much better odds and higher limits to encourage the punters to bet with me. I recruited 'runners', and I paid them a better commission. I opened an account with Guntrips, a national firm with their headquarters in Catford. If I had taken any bets that presented more liability than I could cover, I would hedge with them. I also rang them to update me with the race results. By the late afternoon, I would meet the train from London, and I would buy the early evening papers that contained the full results.

This meant that I could work out the bets and then go off to pay out any winners and take any bets on the evening greyhounds. My main bets were only for a few shillings, but some could run up to quite a high liability. This was because the working man wasn't interested in betting on favourites, but would go for outsiders at long odds, with enough form to give them a chance. When they got lucky, I had to be sure that I could cover it, as it wasn't my nature to 'Welch' on a bet.

Fixed odds football was very popular, and although cash betting of any kind was illegal, there was a back-street printer who would print fixed odds football coupons. Odds were offered for selecting eight home wins, four away winners and three draws. The three draws forecast was a very popular bet. I went to see him, and I arranged to have my own coupons printed.

It became obvious to me that I could not continue to run this business from home. I was never going to make the sort of living that I was looking for, and it was not fair on my mother whose health was never good. My father did not object to my venture, but he did worry that I would 'come a cropper'.

I decided to get an office and I set myself up as a Commission Agent. Bookmakers had to call themselves either commission agents or turf accountants, and take credit bets, to conform to the law. This enabled them to take cash bets under cover. I had some cards printed and I became self-employed. The Inland Revenue weren't concerned whether your business was cash or credit, to them it was all taxable. They required you to submit your audited accounts to them every year.

There were two established bookmakers in Tonbridge. Bob Bert in Priory Road, and Ron Thompson who had a little hut at the back of 'The Gallopers' pub in the High Street.

I looked for somewhere at the opposite end of town and I found a little back-office that had previously been rented by a solicitor. It was next to an Estate Agent and Whites Wine shop, who were the landlords. The manager was a big old boy named Smith. He agreed for me to rent it for a pound per week.

It was situated at the end of a long passage from the front door, and then up a flight of stairs to a small room at the back. There was a washroom and WC downstairs that was shared with all the staff from the Estate Agent. It had electric lighting and two small round pin sockets that could be used to boil a kettle. There was an open fire and the coal was kept in a cupboard under the stairs.

I had a name plate made 'R.J. Saunders Commission Agent 146B 'and I fixed this to the wall outside in the High Street.

I got Den to help me to construct a counter and I bought a second-hand desk and an office chair. There was a telephone socket, so I informed the post office who re-installed the phone and put my number in their directory.

Chapter 9

Jill was nineteen, and by now we knew that we were meant for each other. She had grown into a lovely young woman, with an hourglass figure and thick, naturally wavy auburn hair. We told her parents that we intended to marry, but not until we could afford it, and find our own place to live. Her parents gave us their blessing, but her mother insisted on it being a church wedding.

I told Mum and Dad who were pleased for me, and also Gran and Dusty who were equally pleased. I took Jill to London to buy the engagement ring, and she saw a simple diamond solitaire ring in a jeweller's window. It was Saatchi and Laurence Piccadilly Circus, and it cost twenty-five pounds.

As soon as I had settled into my new office and started trading, Jill left her job and came to work for me. In later years she always joked that she had married her boss.

She soon learned to calculate the stakes on the various combination bets, and I would leave her to answer the phone when I went off to see my 'runners' as I continued taking cash. The credit side of the business grew and with the 'runners' phoning their bets in, it all became half legal.

Credit had its drawbacks as I soon learned. With credit, many people overstretch themselves, and they run up losses that they can't or won't pay. They then leave you without paying and move on to bet with another bookmaker. You lose the money and you lose the client. This is even more galling when you have hedged part of their bets and have to pay this amount to your bookmaker. So, you lose twice.

I remember one afternoon a smartly dressed, well-spoken man coming into the office and asking if he could open an account. He said that he was in Tonbridge on business and that he was staying just across the road in The Rose and Crown Hotel. He said that he'd be here for some time and he was about to move his business here. He convinced me of his credentials, and I agreed.

Later he phoned a small bet which lost and as the afternoon went on, he ran up some more losses. He then wanted to place a large bet on the phone, but I refused it, as he was up to his limit. He said that he would send the hotel porter across with the money, but he could not get here till after the race.

I hesitated, but I knew that if I did not take it that he would probably not pay me the losses he had already accrued. I accepted the bet and it was in the next race. The liability was too much for me, so I had to quickly hedge off the biggest part of it. The horse lost and the hotel porter did not appear.

Believing that I'd been conned, I closed the office and I ran across to the hotel to confront him. Apart from a strange man who had used the phone, they knew nothing about him. That left me out of pocket for the bet that I'd hedged.

It's said that bookmakers never lose. Well if they know their business, this is true over the long-term. But over the short-term they can, and they often do lose, when results go against them. This can go on for quite a long period, and they only survive if they have enough resources to sustain it. I have known quite a few who went broke.

I was always aware that a losing run would make it difficult for me. I needed a guaranteed regular income, so I looked for other ways to ensure this. My football coupons were losing me money, as competition from the big firms was forcing everyone to keep offering higher and higher odds.

I became an agent for William Hill who had a nationwide fixed odds business. I would accept his coupons from punters up till one p.m. on Saturdays and then the area agent, Tim Keating from Brighton, would collect them from me. I also became an agent for both Sherman's and Zetters Pools.

When I had worked with Bob, the Union had a fund-raising ticket lottery that he ran. For sixpence you could buy a little square cardboard ticket with crimped edges. When this was opened it revealed two letters of the alphabet. These had to be matched to the first two letters of the first two words of the headlines in The Daily Mirror. They lasted for that week, and then you had to buy another one for the next week. If the letters matched, you won a pound. For the reverse order you got five shillings. There were also IOU's worth half a crown.

When Bob retired these had ended. The printer who did them was the same old boy who'd printed my fixed odds coupons, so I contacted him. Every Friday evening, he would deliver them to my office, and I'd pay him cash. He suffered with emphysema and I could hear him gasping for breath as he came along the passage and up my stairs. He'd lie across my counter for several minutes, before gasping his way back again.

Come Saturday night, those that I had not sold would be taken around the pubs by my runner, together with the results sheet, so they could check and be paid out there and then. I would give him the IOU tickets separately, so that he could use them to boost interest if no one had won. This was a good little earner and it gave me a cash injection.

**

Mum's depression got worse, and nothing that I or Dad said or did, made her feel better. The doctor recommended that she be put into a mental hospital for treatment, and we persuaded her that she should.

I used to visit her on my motorbike, and she would beg me to take her home. They were giving her electrical treatment and she described how terrible it was. I did not believe her, and I told her that they were trying to help her, and that it was for her own good. It was called 'shock therapy'. An electric shock is used to induce a seizure, that's intended to treat chemical imbalances in the brain. I am surprised to learn now, that this barbaric treatment is still used today. It's called 'Electro Convulsive Therapy', (ECT). I still have it on my conscience that I let her endure such torture.

**

Bookmakers back then tended to be like Damon Runyan characters. Tunbridge Wells had several who could have come straight out of the American prohibition era. I ran up against them occasionally because I collected bets from the railway there. The two bookmakers in Tonbridge, were at the other end of the town, but with my railway connections, I was poaching some of their business. Bob Bert had retired and his son Pete, who'd been in the army at the same time as I, took over.

Ron Thompson was a larger than life guy, who always wore a dark suit and a tie with a black homburg hat. He drove through the town in a big black Oldsmobile. I arranged a meeting with them to discuss business and I convinced them that there was enough to go around for all of us, without cutting each other's throats.

We would meet up one night a week in The Castle Hotel. We'd have a drink and discuss business. There were plenty of clever punters around who would exploit any loophole, and leave one or other of us owing money, and then take their bets to the other.

A little while later, another bookmaker opened an office in Tonbridge High Street opposite Ron Thompson. He was Gordon Chapman, who knew nothing about bookmaking, as he'd come from catering and he owned the Hilden Manor Hotel. He was a pompous character and he made it clear straight away that he intended to take over all the local businesses. Needless to say, we didn't much like him.

One afternoon when I was out, a man came into the office with what was then a very large cash bet. Jill was there and she took it, knowing that I could hedge part of it. It was three five-pound doubles and a five-pound treble on the first, third and last race, second favourites, at Slough Greyhound track.

This seemed a fair enough bet, but I calculated the possible liability and it came to about seven hundred and fifty pounds. That was far too much for me to handle at that time, so I rang Guntrips to hedge it. The girl told me to hang on while she sent for the manager. He came on and he said that they couldn't take it as it was a scam.

At Slough, and at some other provincial dog tracks, on certain nights the starting prices were rigged. The winners were always declared as second favourites. This left me with a problem, and I wondered how many other local bookmakers knew about it.

I went to Jack Neal and I asked him to help me. We split the bet into small separate amounts, so as not to cause suspicion, he then went around on his motorbike and placed these smaller bets with any other bookmakers in the area who would take them. He took the biggest amount to the new bookmaker Gordon Chapman. Sure, enough the bet won and the next day Jack went to collect the winnings. He said that Gordon Chapman had looked at him suspiciously when he paid out.

Before the chap who'd placed the scam with me came for his winnings, I had a phone call from Ron Thompson. He said that his clerk had been stealing from him, and to pay it back he had taken the money from the till and used it for the bet with me. Ron asked me to hold on to it and meet him that night. When we met, he said that his clerk had agreed for me to pay the winnings to Ron.

I gave him the money and I told him what I'd done to cover it. We agreed not to tell the other bookmakers, but Ron was pleased about Gordon Chapman's contribution.

Later that year we all came together, and we formed a local bookmakers association. Ron proposed me and I became secretary.

Den had left his job on the railway and he was the caretaker to the Sussex Road Boys School. This meant that after his morning duties that he was free until the evenings. It also meant that he could come and work for me part time in the afternoons. I would take down the telephone bets from my 'runners' while Jill worked the counter.

I subscribed to a telephone service that I could ring, and Den would chalk up the results, race by race, as we got them.

A teenage jockey named Lester Piggott was causing a sensation in the racing world. The punters loved him, and they would always bet on his big race mounts. I had a 'runner' in Pembury Hospital named Bert Kemp, who was the head porter. He collected all the bets from the staff and the patients, and he phoned them through to me.

In 1954 Lester's Derby mount was a 33 to 1 outsider called 'Never Say Die', and every hospital bet that Bert phoned through to me was on it. I held as much as I could, and when it won, I was stretched to cover all my losses.

When Piggott retired, he had scored nearly four and a half thousand winners and won the Derby no less than nine times. He was tall for a jockey and his balance was so good, he could distribute his weight over the horse's withers, so that the horse hardly knew that he was there. It was reckoned that this was worth a stone less in weight.

***

Mum's condition had worsened, and she was diagnosed with breast cancer. She was admitted into Pembury Hospital and they removed her breast and the lymph glands. It left her terribly scared and it was more like butchery than surgery.

She rapidly declined and Dad and I fixed up a bed for her downstairs in the kitchen. I wrote to the hospital consultant, saying that I was willing to pay for any treatment that might help, but he replied that there was nothing that they could do. They only gave her six months to live. She was in terrible pain and the first doctor who came to see her, Doctor Barlas, said that she was constipated, and he prescribed a laxative. My father was furious, and he could have killed him. After that a Doctor Cooper came to see her and he gave her morphine. She died four months later in October 1954.

Dad and I laid her out and we put her into a clean nightie. I put pennies on her eyelids to keep them closed, as I'd once read that this is what you had to do. I went to see Jill's mother and I asked her if she knew of an undertaker, and what did we have to do.

There were two in Tonbridge High Street and she knew them, so she helped me to arrange the funeral. They came to the house and they took Mum to their chapel and she was buried in Tonbridge Cemetery.

Dad and I would go to the cemetery with flowers every Sunday, and after my visits had fallen off, he still went every Sunday, without fail, for a very long time.

I shall always remember her as a most loving person, who through the very hardest of times, did everything that she could for me. I have very few regrets in my life, but failing to do more for her, is one of them.

I continued with the business, and every afternoon after I closed, I would go home and cook supper. Dad did not get home till late, so sometimes I would light the fire and leave his dinner in the oven. I'd then go back to spend the evening with Jill.

On most Sundays, Jill's Mum would invite my Dad and me to have lunch with them.

We had another runner named George who was an inmate at the Princess Christian's Home in Hildenborough. He would bring their bets in and stay for a chat. Sometimes a doctor from there would also come. He was a big black man who reminded me of Paul Robeson the American singer. He liked to talk, and he said that he had always wanted to go to France.

He would end every sentence saying, "No be so." So, we called him Nobeso.

Dusty used to pop in to see us when he was in town and have a cup of tea.

One day when Jill was there alone, as Dusty was leaving, he saw the doctor coming along the passage. Dusty came back and stood at the counter until the doctor left. He explained to Jill afterwards that he would not leave her alone with a black man. Jill laughed and said that there was nothing to be afraid of as she knew him well.

Sometime later we had a postcard from the doctor in France, and on the back was written, 'Well, well, well, I'm here aren't I'.

Another regular was a former German POW who had married an English girl and had stayed here.

His name was Nofiz and he would start every sentence by saying, "My Christ Mr Saunders I tell you."

There was then a pessimistic middle-aged Welshman who would always have tales of woe and he would end by saying, "You know what I mean Mr Saunders."

We had many customers like that, and it was sometimes more like a social club than a bookmaker's.

At the depot where Jill's dad worked there was a chap who did the cleaning for them. This was Bill Latter who lived in 'The Slade' just around the corner from us. They had a market there once a week and Bill would collect their bets and bring them to me. He also came each evening to sweep up the office, and on Friday nights he'd mop the floors. I paid him a pound per week for this.

I still rented the basement gym, but Deg had gone to Southampton, Den worked with me part-time and Ian had gone to Australia, so it wasn't being used.

Jack Neal had left his job at the ironmongers and he worked for a firm that repaired mowers. He would drive around collecting them and he needed somewhere to store them while they were waiting to be repaired. He'd helped me out, so I returned the favour by letting him use the basement for this. On weekends he would earn himself some extra cash by contract lawn mowing with the machines he'd mended.

Den's mother, a large round woman, would send her bets in with him every day. I'd never known anyone who could stretch a shilling or two to cover so many horses. Her bets were sixpence each way, up and down, any to come on more selections. For a stake of two shillings she could cover bets on twenty horses. She was also very lucky, and it took me ages to work them all out.

I went to his house one evening, and she told me that her eldest son who lived in the top flat above our gym, was moving out. He and his wife had been waiting for a council house and they had finally got one. She suggested that I contact the landlord, as she knew that I was waiting to get married. I knew him, as I was already renting the basement.

Rents were controlled strictly then, and landlords were required to carry out necessary repairs etc. I told him that I would do all the internal decorating and repairs, and he agreed to me having the top flat for a pound a week.

There was no hot water or central heating. The pipes were still made from lead, and the kitchen sink was beside the fireplace, in a cupboard. On the other side was an electric cooker with a piece of aluminium nailed to the wall behind, to act as a splashback. This was painted a sickly green colour.

The bathroom had a bath and a basin, but no hot water. This was obtained by ladling it from a Burco Boiler. The other rooms were better, and I knew that I could improve the flat. It was not like the apartments in the American films that I'd dreamed of, but it was better than where I'd come from and Jill was happy to make it our home.

Jill and I set a date for March 1955, and I meanwhile, set about improving the flat. I fitted an under-sink electric heater for hot water and I tiled the wall behind the cooker. I also fitted an extractor fan and air filter. I went to John Bonner's furniture shop near my office and I purchased a dining room set and a kitchen cabinet. Gran and Dusty bought us a double bed as a wedding present, and her half-brother, Uncle Sid, bought us a dinner service. Dad bought the crockery, and friends gave us other useful items. I hired the Medway Hall for the reception and Jill and her mother made out the guest list.

Jill borrowed her wedding dress from a girl who she used to work with. The only thing new was her veil. We went to see the vicar to arrange for the ceremony, at the Parish Church just across the road from my office in Tonbridge High Street. We did not live in his parish, but by then Gran and Dusty were living in a council flat at the top end of the town, so I gave that as my address.

The day of the wedding was a Saturday, and we got married between races. Jill now had a nine-year-old sister Jacie, who was her bridesmaid, and Deg came up from Southampton to be my best man. Den and another brother, Ted, stayed working at the office, and I left them after the three p.m. race and I went across to the church. After the ceremony, Jill, her family and everyone went to the reception hall, and I went back to the office to finish the afternoon's racing. I joined them later.

Jill's mother 'Dolly' and her elder sister Molly had done all the catering, and I had arranged the entertainment. Jack Woodlands, from the railway, ran a small amateur band, and I hired him and a singer who worked for the Water Board. Uncle Sid played the mouth organ, and Dusty sang and played the spoons and tap danced. Later in the evening I went back to the office to check on the greyhound racing.

Jill and I spent that night and Sunday at the flat, and then I opened the office as usual on Monday morning.

***

I decided that it was time for me to own a car, so I went to London to see a second-hand Sunbeam-Talbot 90 that I fancied. On getting into it, I found it to be cramped. There was an Allard open topped sports car, but they wanted too much for it.

Back in Tonbridge there was a garage at the top of Priory Road run by a man named Wilcox; a pleasant man, he always addressed me as 'master'. He had a black second hand 14 horsepower Lea-Francis sports saloon, and he offered me a deal. It had an aluminium body built on a wooden chassis, Girling mechanical brakes, built-in jacks on all four wheels and big chrome headlights. The interior had Venetian blinds.

The engine leaked oil, so I sent it up to Charles Follett, the main dealers in London and had it re-bored. The engine was then so tight that the battery would not start it, so it had to be cranked by hand. When it backfired, the starting handle would nearly break your arm.

The braking was also erratic, as the mechanical rods to the front wheels were balanced through a compensator, which sometimes applied different pressure to one side. They were also worn, and they used to rattle over bumpy roads. There were no MOTs in those days.

***

Dad was living on his own in Vale Road, and Monday and Fridays he would not get home from work until after seven p.m. Jill would cook him a meal in our flat, and then we'd take it down and wait for him. I bought him a small convector heater that the electric wiring could just cope with, and we'd put this on, so that the house wasn't freezing when he got in.

As time went by, he was delayed more and more, so he told us not to wait, and he said that he'd warm the dinner up when he got home.

I found out later that he was friendly with the widow who ran the small shop at the top of the road, where he bought his cigarettes. Her name was Olive Hemsley, and he eventually moved in with her. Whether he ever ate the dinners that Jill cooked for him I do not know.

On a quiet racing week, I decided to take Jill on a belated honeymoon. We went to Torquay and we took Gran and Dusty with us. On the way, on a wet downhill road, a milk float pulled out in front of me. I had to brake hard, resulting in a sideways skid that I steered out of, zigzagging down the hill. After that, as we approached Torquay, we went down a very steep hill with a sharp bend at the bottom and Gran said, "Go back Ray."

We stayed with a Mrs Metcalfe who ran a B&B in the town. It cost 12/6d per person per night. On arrival, Gran apologised to her, because Dusty sang in his sleep.

That night Jill and I had been woken up, not by Dusty's singing, but by Gran's snoring. It was like a rip saw and although they were further along the corridor, we could hear it almost rattling the windows. We lay there, laughing at it for a long time. Early the next morning, a young couple with a motorbike and sidecar got up and left.

116

We took them to the caves at Kents Cavern, Cockington, with its thatched cottages and, Gran's favourite, Daddyhole Plain. After that, they would go every year by train, and Dusty found a pub close by where he could play darts despite his limited vision.

***

There was talk of cash betting being legalised, and although this did not come until later in 1961, the attitude towards it had become very relaxed. I installed a ticker tape machine that continually fed all the racing information needed for running the afternoon betting. Jill would take the bets at the counter, while Den would call out the odds and chalk up the results on a large blackboard. I sat at the telephone, kept the book and worked out the winning bets. If you've seen a film called 'The Sting' with Paul Newman and Robert Redford, this will give you an idea of how it was.

The company that supplied this information was The Exchange Telegraph. The engineer who serviced my machine told me that he also serviced one in Clarence House that the Queen Mother had installed. He said that she had a credit account with William Hill. She was a keen follower of National Hunt racing and she owned several racehorses. Her trainer was Peter Cazalet at Fairlawne, close to me in Tonbridge.

The stable used to bet with me, and the stable lads would come to the office. Her jockey, Dick Francis, who later became the famous novelist, also came in sometimes. I cannot be sure, but I think that Major Cazalet came one day to see for himself.

She owned a horse called Devon Loch that was a 100 to 7 (14-1) outsider for the 1956 Grand National. It was trained at Fairlawne.

The Grand National was the biggest betting race of the year and practically the whole nation would have a bet. The result could determine your profitability or otherwise, for the whole year. We could hardly cope with the volume of bets for her horse, right up to the off. Although I'd hedged some, I did not think that the horse could win, so I left myself over stretched. I put the radio on in the office to listen to the commentary while I sat at the desk. It was given by Raymond Glendenning the BBC sports commentator. Coming up to the last fence Devon Loch was in the lead. Clearing the fence, it galloped towards the line well clear. Glendenning was shouting, "Devon Loch is well clear — the Queen Mother is going to win the Grand National, there's only forty-five yards to go."

I snapped my pencil and I said, "That's it, I've lost everything, the car will have to go."

The next thing Glendenning screamed, "ITS DOWN the Queen Mothers horse has fallen with less than forty-five yards to go." He kept repeating it in disbelief. The Irish horse ESB went on to win.

I could hardly believe it. I'd been saved at the post. It is still not known to this day, why the horse went down spread-eagled.

The jockey was mystified, and everyone offered a theory. Some said it was exhausted, others that it tried to jump a shadow, and many more … I only know, that if ever there was a 'Fickle Finger of Fate' moment, that was it.

After that I never again allowed my judgement to overstretch my resources and I made sure that no matter how little chance I thought a horse had of winning, that I covered myself from taking too big a hit.

Gran, hop picking in Kent.

Gran with her sister, Fan', on the farm where we would go at night to steal vegetables

Mum and me with our spaniel puppy, Chum, who died of distemper.

Our mongrel, Bruce, who I slept with in the coal hole under the stairs
during the Blitz.

Mum, me, Dusty, Dad and a playmate on the rocks at Pett Level.

Dusty and Dad shrimping while Gran watches.

Gran shrimping at Pett Level, Kent. Later she would cook them for tea
at the beach chalet.

Me, Gran and Dusty at the beach chalet they hired in summer.

Mum in the 1930s, before her illness.

Dad (left) working on the railway as a chainman, carrying out tunnel examination.

1947, passing my driving test in North Wales.

1948, my mucker, Nobby Clarke.

My quad, gun and limber, Eagle Troop 23rd Regiment RA.

Me with Jack Neal on his Velocette OHC.

Charlie Oughton with me and Jill at Brands Hatch.

The four musketeers.
Left to right, Ken, me, Deg and Den at Eastbourne.

Jill is not the only pebble on the beach, but the only one for me.

Deg and me display our hand balancing routine.

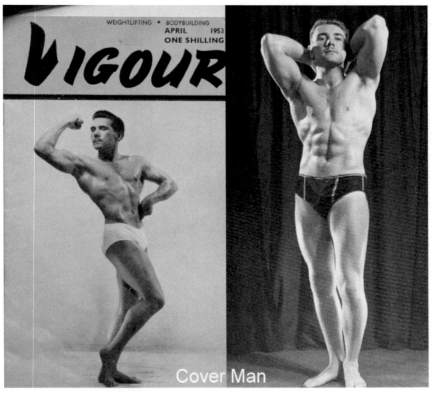

After winning a body building competition, aged twenty-two, I was selected as a cover man for *Vigour* magazine.

Our wedding day in March 1955.

We waited several years before we took our honeymoon in Torquay,
and then took Gran and Dusty with us.

Silver City car ferry service from Lydd to France took twenty minutes
and you were driving off with little formality.

Jack Wells buys his alpenhorn in Interlaken.

My maternal grandfather, Dusty, who was a great influence in my life.
A great character who, aged eighty and registered blind, got a job with
the local council as a lollipop man!

Teaching the stallion to pee in the bucket.

The stallion is not really laughing. His olfactory nerves detect the
mare's oestrogen, causing his lips to curl.

Above: Hubi in an exercise canter.

Left: After his death aged twenty, the BAHS published his photo on the cover of their winter magazine, together with a poem I had written on his life.

Jill and me living the good life.

Still working in the garden we created.

Chapter 10

Jill and I weren't interested much in television, but we bought Gran and Dusty their first TV and we would go to their flat some evenings if there was a programme that we wanted to see.

Dusty's sight had been deteriorating for some time, and I had taken him to Tunbridge Wells Hospital to have cataracts removed. Unfortunately, they found that because of his constant exposure to the sun, that the retinas had also been damaged. This left him with only peripheral vision. He was registered as a blind person.

However, he did not let it stop him from doing things. Their flat had a coal fire and he used to sweep the chimney regularly. A spinster, Miss Hunter, in the next flat kept pestering him to sweep hers. He did not want to but in the end, he gave in. It had not been swept for a long time and there was lots of soot. He put the soot into a sack but as he picked it up, the bottom of the sack burst. The soot spilled out all over the carpet and it also filled her slippers.

When he told me about it afterwards, he said, "If you don't want to do something, make a bad job of it and they won't ask you again."

He saw a job advertised for a school crossing keeper and went to apply for it at the Council. He got the job and we would see him with his lollipop, holding up the traffic for the children to cross. They loved him and would bring him gifts.

I have a photo of him dressed in a long white coat, wearing a peaked cap, and holding the lollipop pole with the stop sign. I can't recall how long he did it, but because of his restricted vision, I don't think that Health and Safety would now agree to a registered blind man being in charge of a children's crossing. It's just as well that the traffic was lighter then.

When he went in for his operation, I left the office to go and visit him, and as I stepped into the street it was snowing hard. I stood under the bus shelter waiting for it to ease. The shelter was a large cantilever type with an asbestos roof supported by concrete pillars. A bus came along and slid into the curb hitting the shelter, which collapsed on top of me. It knocked me flat and the concrete pillar was on top of my chest preventing me from getting up. Who should come along but my friend Ken Woolley. He helped me up and he took me back to my office.

Jill phoned for an ambulance and they took me to hospital. I had an X-Ray taken, and nothing was broken. I was bruised and my trench coat was ruined.

Even today, I still sometimes feel the effect of it in my ribcage, if I turn awkwardly. Now it would be a case for compensation, but back then it was just an unfortunate accident.

Paddock Wood was a small town nearby and there were no bookmakers there. There were two main businesses, Smedley's, the fruit canning factory, and Halls, who made timber buildings. Commercial Road was the main road for shops, and this led to the railway station. It was also the main centre for fruit picking and hop picking, that drew lots of Londoners during the season. I decided that it would be a good place to open another office.

Opposite the canning factory was a bakery shop, and behind it was an empty bakehouse. It was Accott's Bakery and I went to see Mr Accott. He agreed to rent me the bakehouse building. I bought some hardboard sheets and timber from a dealer in Tonbridge, and Jack Neal used his van to help me get it to Paddock Wood. We had to tie the lengths of timber on top, and on the way, it slipped off and hung over the near side. Jack was going fast and swerved, but how it managed to miss hitting a row of telegraph poles I'll never know. Jack being his normal self just made a joke of it. He helped me erect a partition at one end and we made a counter. It had electricity but if you needed a WC it meant going into the shop.

I offered Den a regular job in my Tonbridge office, and he came to work for me full time. I would go to Paddock Wood each day and I would be open from eleven a.m. till two p.m. I would then go back to Tonbridge to join Jill and Den for the afternoon's racing. It worked well as it covered the lunchtime period and the workers soon got to know that they could easily have a bet there.

Later, I employed a woman to take the bets and I would collect her at two p.m. and then return to Tonbridge.

One day, when driving through Tonbridge High Street I spotted Dusty pushing a cart loaded with logs. They had moved to a Council bungalow in Chestnut Walk at the far end of town. Dusty would go to the Baltic Sawmills in Lyons Crescent and buy logs. For 2/6d you could have as many as you liked, so he would pile the cart up to its full capacity.

I could not stand to watch him struggle all that way, so I parked my car and I pushed it home for him. I wondered what it would do for my image, if my punters saw their bookmaker pushing a cartload of logs through the town.

We did not need to open the Tonbridge office until 10.30 a.m. So, in the summer we would go swimming every morning. We also went regularly to Sevenoaks to the Bradbourne Riding Centre, run by Peter Felgate. He was a very good instructor and I enjoyed taking part in his cross-country events.

I'd given up the weight training and instead I took up tennis. Jill could already play. On the Tonbridge Sports Ground there were several public grass courts that could be hired, and we would play there together with Den, June Millson and another of Jill's school friends, Sheila Woolley and her husband Ken.

There were several clubs that rented some of the courts for their exclusive use. I contacted the Council and I rented one and I formed our own club. Later I joined the UNA club and I transferred our equipment over to them. This gave us the opportunity to play to a much higher standard, including the Kent league.

I took lessons from Major Price who was a member of the LTA and who coached at the Sacred Heart School in Tunbridge Wells.

I always finished second in the club singles championship, beaten by Jackie Luff. We had to play after work in the evenings, and in one final it took us three evenings over three long sets. I lost the last set 15–17.

I could never master top spin and I was a flat hitter of the ball. Also, most club tennis was mixed doubles and I much preferred singles matches.

Ken Woolley and I began playing squash at the Hilden Manor. I soon became good, as my flat hitting and quick reflexes produced good results. Ken arranged a match between me and the captain of the Nottingham

University Squash Team. They were top of the University league at the time. He was twenty and I was ten years older. I lost to him after three close sets.

Another friend, Ken Eaton was keen on fencing and he was a member of a club that fenced at the Tonbridge School. He got permission for us to use their squash courts. We all played there, and Jill would play against Ken Woolley's wife Sheila.

One night I was playing against Ken Woolley, and as he swung at the ball his racket struck me across the bridge of the nose. The force broke the racket and blood poured out of my nose. Ken, who suffered from asthma, then had an attack. I could not stop the bleeding, so they insisted that I went to a doctor.

At the surgery, the doctor said that he would not stitch it as it would leave a tuck. He stuck a plaster over it. Two weeks later it had festered, and when I pulled the plaster off, out came a piece of wood from his racket shaft. I still have the scar.

When the Professional Tennis Championships were on at Wembley, I would obtain tickets. Jill would pack some sandwiches and a flask, and I would drive up after we closed the office. There was no trouble parking and during the interval we'd sit and eat our sandwiches. Pancho Gonzales, Lew Hoad, Kenny Rosewall and all the great pro players would compete. Jill's favourite was the American Tony Trabbert. We also went to Eastbourne once to watch the great Rod Laver.

Ken Eaton was also keen on surfing and he introduced me to it. It was not sophisticated as it is now, just plain wooden boards for body surfing.

We went down to Newquay on holiday together with another couple, Jack and Joy Bryant. Jack was an insurance collector, he had a great sense of humour and we called him 'The Jolly Swag Man'. Jill and I only had a week and we stayed on the main road outside the town. It was a B&B run by a Mrs Kessell for 17/6d a night pp. There was a manhole in the road outside our bedroom window, and the cover would clonk loudly every time a car went over it.

The other four stayed at a small hotel in the town. Ken moaned all the week about the food and their bedroom and he said that he would not stay on after the week was up and Jack and Joy had left.

When they came to pay the woman said, "You've booked another week Mr. Eaton, and as it comes into the busy season it will cost you more."

Ken sheepishly agreed, much to the other two's amusement

***

I changed my car for a little Austin A40 estate. Some Saturday nights we would leave the office and I would pick up Ken and Joyce. We'd load up all the stuff, including the surfboards and food, and also two airbeds and a ridge tent.

I would drive down to Westward Ho so that we could have a day's surfing, and then drive back Sunday night. It was about two hundred and forty miles each way.

One night we'd pulled into a layby around midnight, and we were just preparing to kip down, when the headlights of another car drew up right behind us.

Joyce said, "Fancy him parking right there."

A big police sergeant then got out and said, "You cannot stay here."

We said that we did not know as it was our first time.

He said, "They all say that."

After some discussion he agreed to us staying, provided that we were gone by first light.

When he drove off, Ken set about erecting the ridge tent, and I blew up the airbeds, for Jill and Joyce to sleep on in the car. Ken used meat skewers to fix down the tent, and as he tried to knock them in, they kept bending. He then discovered that what looked like grass in the dark, was only moss covering the tarmac.

Eventually we settled down inside, but it was so narrow that we were squeezed against the sides.

We were in sleeping bags, and just as I was about to doze off, Ken said, "It's no good, I'm too hot. I will have to take my socks off."

This manoeuvre caused the tent to partially collapse on top of us. It then started raining and the tent leaked. I heard a distant car approaching, and as it came nearer, the noise got louder until it roared past, causing the damn tent to flap against my face.

***

The next morning dawned bright and fine and Ken cooked breakfast on his spirit stove. We had camped right alongside an old churchyard and Joyce said that she would not have slept if she had known.

The surfing was good, but it was very windy and when Ken came out and struggled up the pebble bank with his surfboard, his eyes were bloodshot, and he was blue all over. There were no wetsuits in those days.

Later in a faster car, I drove to Newquay and back in a day. We left on Sunday at four a.m. and we were on Perranporth Beach by ten thirty. We spent the day surfing. We had a meal in the beach café. We left at seven p.m. and got home at two a.m. on Monday morning. A total round trip just short of six hundred miles. We then opened the office as usual. When we were surfing, someone said to Jill that it was a better day than yesterday. Jill did not like to say that we had driven all that way for a day, so she agreed that it was.

***

The Odeon Cinema Leicester Square re-opened after fourteen years, with a film called 'Gigi'. I drove up with Jill, Joyce and Ken, to see it, and we parked right outside. When Maurice Chevalier finished singing 'I'm glad I'm not young anymore', the audience stood up and clapped. I have never seen that happen before or since.

Jill and I would often go up in the evening to the West End to see a film or more often a show. Afterwards, we would have a late supper at an Italian restaurant. Parking was never a problem.

***

Jack Wells had served as a Flight Engineer during the Italian campaign. He had married Jill's cousin who had died in childbirth, and Jack had remarried. He had an engineering business in Dartford. We met at a family gathering and we became good friends. We would all go out to dinner together and Jack's favourite tipple was Asti Spumante, so we always drank that, whatever the meal was.

141

The singer, Dorothy Squires, opened a restaurant called 'The Starlight Roof' and Jack got tickets for the opening night. It was a posh affair, and we turned up in dress suits and all the ladies wore evening gowns. At one end of the dining room there was an open kitchen with a counter, and on the wall behind was a large painted mural. There was a long delay before our orders were taken and when the chef eventually arrived, he was drunk.

The waitress came around for our orders and the chef began cooking on a large barbeque grill, the flames of which got higher and higher as he threw the meat on. He muddled up the orders, resulting in them being sent back, to which he responded by throwing the plates under the counter.

As the flames got higher the mural began melting and all the paint ran down the wall. The roof was then slid back, and we watched as the smoke and fumes escaped out the top. Eventually the manager and two others came in and bungled him off, and the manager took over the cooking. Meanwhile I went around to all the tables taking bets on when they'd get their dinner. I think it was midnight before the last one was served.

***

Jack and his wife Vera had an Alsatian dog called Cobber and they would go walking in the Lake District. Jill and I would sometimes join them for a couple of days. He was a camera enthusiast and he always had the latest model.

One day, crossing a bog with steppingstones, Jack's latest camera slipped off his shoulder and fell into the mud. He went to step back to retrieve it, but instead he stepped on it pushing it down into the bog. We walked on to the next village and we found a little general store. Jack put the camera down on top of the counter and he asked the chap if he sold methylated spirits. He nodded, and Jack asked for three bottles.

The bloke went off and when he came back, he put them down on the counter. Jack then asked for a bucket and this was brought and placed beside the bottles. Jack paid, and as the bloke stood looking, Jack emptied the meths into the bucket and he proceeded to dunk the camera up and down in it. He then thanked the bloke and we walked out leaving the bloke looking utterly bewildered. Jack explained to me that the spirit would clean out the water and when the camera dried that it would be fine. Actually, it was not, so he sent it to Japan to be repaired and he ended up paying more than the cost of a new one.

When the new polaroid cameras came out Jack had one and he used to put the film under his arm to develop it.

***

When I could get away, I would go down to Exmoor to a riding centre run by the Lamacraft's. Edgar, the father, and his wife Dorothy had a riding business for many years in Dunster. They had recently joined forces with their son John, and they had bought another property. They had forty or more horses and they ran holidays for hunting or adventure rides on Exmoor.

We became very friendly and I would go hunting with Edgar, while Jill would ride out with John and the others. Edgar was an old-time horseman and I learned a lot from him.

He had put his age down and he had joined the Veterinary Corps in World War Two. He was sent to Ireland to buy some young horses for the Army. He told me that Army horses always had their number tattooed on their gums. When he inspected those for sale, some numbers showed that they'd been recruited for the First World War.

Jack and Vera would also come down. Jack was top heavy and couldn't ride well. It didn't put him off though and he was always game for a challenge.

One day we'd all been on a day ride and coming back at lunchtime we stopped at a pub in Porlock. We tied the horses up in the skittle alley and then we had a boozy lunch. Edgar would buy one of the locals a pint to clean up the droppings afterwards.

Returning home along the lane, Jack said that he'd have to spend a penny. I stayed back with him while the others rode on. Jack got off and he began urinating into a bed of stinging nettles. The horse then lowered its head and it gave Jack a push in the back, that sent him sprawling into the nettles. I could not stop laughing. Jack then could not get back onto the horse. There was a farm gate there, so I told him to climb onto it and then he could mount. He did, and just as he'd cocked one leg over the horse's back, it walked away, and Jack fell down again. I almost fell off laughing.

He could not do the rising trot keeping in rhythm with the horse and he would bump up and down. He said you never see cowboys bobbing up and down, so he had bought a western saddle. The leather was very stiff, so they told him to smother it in oil to soften it.

The first time he used it, the stirrup leathers kept stretching. Coming back along the lane, Jack's stirrups had dropped so much that he was balancing most uncomfortably on his crotch.

Word came up through the line that Jack had said, "For God sake don't start trotting."

On another occasion we were galloping through a wood and we all ducked under the tree branches. Jack did not see them in time and one bough swiped him off.

Not being able to get back on, Edgar said, "Git 'e in the ditch, Jack."

Instead of putting the horse in the ditch so that he was level with it, Jack went down and stood in it.

Edgar said, "You do like making things bloody difficult for yourself."

***

In all our married life Jill rarely asked me to buy her anything.

If she admired something, I would say, "Would you like me to buy it for you."

She would say, "No, just because I like it does not mean that I want it."

Of course, this did not stop me from buying her things. She was a contented person and she was happy with the simple things in life.

On one visit to the Lake District, I saw a long white sheepskin coat in a shop window in Bowness. It looked very fashionable and it was trimmed in leather with leather buttons. It was seventy-five pounds and I said that I should buy it for her. Jill agreed and we went in and bought it.

Vera was just the opposite. If she saw someone with something that she liked; she would want one too. She insisted that Jack bought her one, but she was unlucky as it was a one-off. It meant that Jack was in the doghouse for the rest of our stay.

***

The Transport Minister Ernest Marples was opening the M1 motorway and Jack wanted to be one of the first to use it. He went up and stayed at the same hotel as the Minister. We had arranged to meet up there the following morning. When we arrived, there had been a fire in the night and the hotel had burnt down. They said that everyone was okay and they had been transferred to another hotel.

We went to find them, and Vera told us what had happened. She had been awoken in the night by Cobber scratching at the door. She could smell smoke and she could hear the noise of people in the corridor. Their bedroom lights went off and she panicked and woke Jack. He never wore pyjamas, preferring to sleep in the nude. He grabbed the first thing that he found which was his V-necked pullover. Thrusting his legs through the armholes he ran out into the corridor.

The Minister's aides were running up and down with his luggage, and Jack was waving to them to shut the doors so as not to feed oxygen to the fire. Vera grabbed Cobber and when she got there, she found that Jack had pulled the pullover on to cover his body, but with the 'V' at the front! The hotel charged them for the night and the other hotel charged them for breakfast.

***

I took Jill to a Bentall's store in Kingston. It was before Christmas and we were shopping for presents. In the middle of one floor there was a display of glass and crystal. The centrepiece was a large 14" crystal bowl. There had been a big exhibition in Germany where this had been featured, and Bentall's had acquired it for their Christmas display.

Jill said, "If you want to buy me something, I'd really like that crystal bowl."

It wasn't priced, and when I insisted that I'd like to buy it the girl said that she'd have to fetch the manager. He said that he could not sell it, but I'm nothing if not persistent when I want something. In the end he agreed, and he sold it to me for twenty-five pounds.

***

It sparked my interest to find out more about it. It was Dr Johnson's Bowl and it was made by Thomas Webb. Long since taken over, back then they made the finest crystal in the world and their lead content was the highest. I wrote to Thomas Webb, telling them of my acquisition and they invited me to their factory in Stourbridge. The four of us went up in Jack's car, and as we drove up the M1 we listened to the radio. It was a commentary of John Glenn as he became the first American astronaut to orbit the earth. As we covered fifty miles or so, he had passed over Africa.

On arriving in Birmingham there was no accommodation to be had anywhere. There was a big conference on, and all the hotels were booked solid. Jack was a member of the AA and we went to their headquarters to see if they could help. They tried but they could not find anything. The clerk said that he'd be there all night and he offered to let us sleep in the lounge armchairs. I remember that it was cold, and Jack gave Vera his sheepskin coat. He was very overweight and he never seemed to feel the cold. The next morning, we used their washroom to wash and to shave, and we then went to the factory.

The manager took us around the works, showing us every stage of the manufacturing process. Their crystal used the most lead, and Australian white sand. This gave it the finest purity and quality. Founded in 1829, the process had hardly changed, and I was astonished to see that the glass blowers actually blew these large bowls, holding the molten glass at the end of a long tube.

While we watched this being done, one of the men took a blob of liquid glass and he shaped it into three little figures like swans, and they presented them to Jill. I learned that their standard bowls were twelve inches and that our Dr Johnson's bowl being fourteen inches, was one of only three that they made every year. These mostly went to the States.

We watched them being engraved where they were handheld against a large revolving stone wheel. The engraving of the Wellington design of ours, could take up to two weeks to cut. They said that as the crystal cooled it formed stress lines and if the engraver cut through them the bowl could shatter. This was why they made so few. We were also told that when you buy crystal you can often see bubbles in it. They said not to worry as this was caused by the lead and that it was a mark of good quality.

Chapter 11

Cash betting was finally legalised in 1961 by the then Chancellor 'Rab' Butler. Bookmakers were licensed and their offices could then be used to take cash bets but could not be advertised. To obtain a licence, you had to prove to the court that you were 'a fit and proper person' and that you had no criminal record. You were also required to satisfy the court that you had enough resources to maintain a cash betting business, and that you had enough experience to cope with it.

Before going to court the magistrates, together with the chief of police, spent an afternoon in my office watching me conduct illegal cash betting, to prove that I could cope with it when it became legal.

It was widely suspected that this was the forerunner of the introduction of a betting tax, and that the big firms were manoeuvring for representation in Parliament.

Locally I called a meeting of our bookmakers association and we decided to expand our representation to cover a larger area. At a meeting with the Maidstone bookmakers it was decided to form The West Kent Bookmakers Association and they voted me in as secretary.

I went with a delegation to London where Ladbrokes and Coral had arranged to meet with the MP Bob Mellish, to get him to speak on behalf of the bookmakers.

After the first meeting, I and the other smaller groups dropped out, and it was left to Cyril Stein and Joe Coral to carry the flag. Whether or not they persuaded the MP to speak on their behalf I do not know. William Hill was not there as he had no interest in cash betting and he did not open any offices. Soon there were ten thousand cash betting shops in the country. Locally there were regular applicants for a licence.

Representing the established bookmakers, I would attend the court hearings to protest to any being granted, as the area was already adequately served. One applicant always beat me, and it puzzled me as I had a strong case.

Someone then said to me, "Look at the tie he wears."

I realized then that he always wore a military tie and that the magistrates were all retired army officers.

***

Parking restrictions were introduced in the town, and traffic wardens were recruited. One of them named Vince was particularly enthusiastic and he was hated by everyone.

I parked in a twenty-minute zone outside a shoe shop and I went in with Jill. Before the time was up, I left, and I told her that I would pick her up later. When I returned, I parked in the same spot while I went in to collect her.

I thought no more of it until I received a parking fine. I was very annoyed and on reading the summons I noticed that the last two numbers of my number plate were in reverse order.

I rang my solicitor intending for him to challenge it for me. He was the senior partner of the firm and he asked if I had parked there. I said yes, but not for the total time stated, as I'd left and returned later. I said then that my number plate was misquoted. He thought that it was near enough and that it would be easiest to just pay the fine as it was not much. This riled me and I decided that I'd defend it myself.

I contacted the car registration department and I found out that the number quoted on the summons belonged to a man in Maidstone. I rang him and I asked him if his car was the same make as mine, it wasn't. It was the same colour though. Furthermore, he had not been in Tonbridge on the day in question, so I could not use that as a case of mistaken identity.

I rang Cobley's, a men's outfitters in the town, and I asked them if they stocked military ties. They confirmed that they did. I asked if they had one for the Royal Artillery Regiment and they said they had. It was 16/9d and I told them to save it for me.

On the day of the court hearing I turned up and I told them that I was pleading not guilty and that I was defending myself. They said that in that case, I could either just make a statement from the back of the court, or I could take the stand and be questioned. Afterwards I could then question the witness. I chose the latter.

The council's solicitor put their case that I'd overrun the time limit and he asked me about it. I told him I had not. I then stood down and I called the traffic warden to the stand. He had produced his notebook as proof of my stay, and I asked him to read out the number of my car.

It then suddenly occurred to me that maybe he had got it right, but the summons had misquoted it. However, all was well, and he read out the wrong number.

I asked him if he was sure that he had the right number and he said, "Yes."

I said, "Are you quite sure."

"Yes," he responded.

I then turned to the magistrates and I told them that this was not my number, and that it belonged to a man in Maidstone. I then produced my logbook as evidence. They did not ask if the other man had been in town that day and they dismissed the case. I went home and I put the tie in the wardrobe for another day. I wore it every time in court after that.

There were some local villains in the area who were suspected of having been involved in a robbery in Matfield, but the police could not prove it. Later they were involved in a robbery in Southampton, where a customs officer had been killed. This resulted in prison sentences for two of them.

One of the others had his premises dug up by detectives from London, after a murder. The police called them the mini Kray gang.

My office at Paddock Wood was vandalised twice and the electrical supply ripped out. I reported it to the police, and they said that they thought they knew who was responsible. They fitted an alarm system that was connected directly to their Maidstone response room, so that if it happened again, they could act quickly. They even came to my home to check my security.

It did happen again, but the alarm did not work. As those they suspected, had prison records, I knew that they would not be able to get a betting license. I thought that they were acting for a third party, and I had a pretty good idea who it was. I'd been told by my punters that there was someone approaching them to bet with him. I would not be intimidated, and I stuck it out until it stopped.

***

William Hill fixed odds football coupons were very popular, and the odds kept increasing because of the intense rivalry with Ladbrokes. They ran a competition to see which of their agents could increase their turnover the most. It coincided with my gaining a client who was a fruit farmer who laid out a lot of money on his football bets. I had a letter from Hill to say that I'd won and that I could choose the first prize. We did not have a fridge, so we chose a Hotpoint and it lasted for many years.

On busy afternoons with the office in full swing, you could hardly see across the counter for cigarette smoke. I installed two extractor fans in the ceiling and when I cleaned the filters it scraped off like tar. The white ceiling went brown.

Fridays were always busy and sometimes we would get the Irish labourers in, who were working on local building sites. They were paid on Friday and when the pubs turned out at two p.m. they would come to bet on the afternoon's racing. Often, they'd be drunk, but they were usually not much trouble.

Unlike today, bad language wasn't used much and if it was, I would quickly point out that there was a lady present and shut them up. Sometimes one would get boisterous and I would bundle him off down the stairs, march him along the passage and leave him lying over the bus stop barrier outside.

***

Our flat in Baltic Road was part of an old Victorian house, built in 1899 by a master builder named Casper Jarvis. It had a double bay windowed front and it was divided into two parts. On one side was a semi-detached three bedroomed house, and the other had been made into two flats plus a basement. It was built on the side of a hill so that the front was two stories and the back was three.

151

Originally it was the only house there, built on what was then the St. Stevens Park Estate. I wrote to the owner, a nice old chap named Faith, asking him if he would be interested in selling, and he came to see me at the office. He was quite keen to sell as he was getting on, and it was becoming a burden to him.

He was worried because the Labour party was threatening to take over all private landlords if they won the next election, and he also wanted to pay off the mortgage.

I bought it for two thousand pounds. I took over the private mortgage of seven hundred pounds at five percent. I borrowed seven hundred pounds from my bank and I wrote a cheque for the other six hundred pounds. I was now the owner, with two sitting tenants. Mr and Mrs Glover in the lower flat, and Mr and Mrs Wicket next door. They were both on a protected tenancy with a restricted rent of a pound per week. I had the back bedroom of the semi, converted into a bathroom and WC for the old couple, and I set about improvements to my flat.

Later the rent restrictions were gradually lifted, and a yearly inspection was made to assess what would be a fair rent. The rent officer made an assessment, but any increases could only be made in yearly stages. My tenants were both on benefits so they weren't any worse off when their rents went up.

***

During the quiet racing periods I would leave Den in charge and take a few days off and go somewhere riding. Jill and I would pack our riding gear and go wherever riding was advertised. I saw an advert for riding in Scotland. It was at a hotel beside Loch Awe. It was run by two sisters named McTavish, and I booked a week.

The day that we drove up the weather conditions were awful and by the time we got there, it was dark. It was a remote place and I could not find it. I drove for what seemed like miles along a narrow track; the rain so heavy that the wipers struggled to cope. Thunder and lightning, with lashing rain, made it difficult to see ahead, and I stopped the car and I told Jill that we should go back.

In the distance I saw a faint light and the next moment there was a knock on the side window. Peering at me through the glass was a little woman wearing a sou'wester and holding a lantern. I wound the window down and in a thick Scottish accent she asked if I was Mr Saunders.

I said that I was, and she said, "If you hurry, you'll be in time for dinner."

There was a roaring fire inside, with two other people standing there, a Doctor Thompson and his wife. The sister who had met us outside had disappeared, and the other sister came in with a tray and a bottle of sherry. She poured us a glass each and said that dinner would be served in ten minutes. She wore lace up boots, a long black skirt and an old shawl.

The doctor told us that he was going stag shooting the next day and he had booked a gillie. A hand bell sounded, and we went through to dinner. The same sister served us but she was now dressed in a waitress outfit. The dinner was a pleasant surprise and it had a taste of ginger.

***

The next morning, I looked around our bedroom, and on one wall I noticed a handwritten notice. It read 'do not attempt to open this cupboard door'. The wood panelling had been papered over, and if you looked closely you could just make out the outline of a door. There was a bell on the bedside table, and one by the basin close to the window.

Having a shave, I glanced out of the window and I saw that there was a sloping corrugated tin roof. On the wall was another handwritten notice which read, 'in the event of fire open the window and slide down the roof'.

Going down to breakfast there were handbells everywhere marked 'fire alarm'. We helped ourselves to fruit then in came a cooked breakfast, but everything had ginger in it. Sister number two served us and she said that the day's programme was on the duty rota board in the hall.

When we looked it was a list of the day's activities. At ten a.m. Doctor Thompson was deer stalking with a Gillie. We were pony trekking with a guide. It then went on to list the times for lunch. afternoon tea and dinner, I got the feeling that they'd lived in the Indian Raj and were the daughters of a British colonel who'd returned to Scotland and were rather down at heel but trying to emulate their former life.

At precisely ten a.m. the gillie was there and so was sister number two, dressed in Scottish tweeds and high lace-up boots.

Our guide was sister number one now, in old fashioned riding gear, including riding britches that stuck out each side, carrying a hunting crop. We trekked over moors and hills in Scottish mist that soaked everything. I had never ridden a highland pony, being used to blood animals, and I found the plodding tedious. The ponies had long thick hair and steam rose up from them. If you've ever smelt a wet dog, multiply it twenty times.

I told Jill that I could not put up with it, that I felt sorry for them, but we should leave. She agreed and I paid them for a week, we left after two days. I must say that the afternoon teas of homemade scones and jam were very nice, provided you liked ginger.

Chapter 12

Jack Wells grew his engineering business and became friendly with a procurement officer for the Admiralty in Portsmouth. Jack obtained government contracts and he once told me that he was making spares for battleships that had been sunk during the First World War.

He bought a Ford Zephyr saloon and he converted it into an estate car. His design became the forerunner of the big Ford Estate cars.

In June 1962 we decided to take a week's holiday in Switzerland and the four of us went in his car to Interlaken. Jack drove through the night and Jill and Vera slept in the back. Many French towns had cobbled roads and the vibration kept them awake.

Needing a pee, we stopped at a village, and the girls said that their toilet was a concrete block with a hole in the middle with just a recess each side to plant your feet. When daylight came it was raining and we stopped under a railway bridge and Vera cooked breakfast of bacon, eggs and fried bread.

We booked in at the Hotel Krebs in the centre of Interlaken. That night at dinner, the waiter said that we would have to cook our dinner ourselves. He then came back, and to our surprise, he set up a fondue bourguignonne. This was a new experience for us.

After several bottles of wine and of course brandy I went off, and when I came back, I told them that I had ordered a landau for midnight. These horse drawn carriages drove the tourists around the town. The driver put a blanket over our legs, and we set off. Halfway into the tour, Vera, a true animal lover, said that she felt sorry for the horse and she told Jack to get out and walk.

There was a souvenir shop opposite the hotel called 'Salvatorie' and Jack said not to buy anything until our last day. We all went in, and when we asked Salvatorie the price for anything, he replied, "The PRR-ICE is the same."

When we left the shop, Vera and I had bought cuckoo clocks, music boxes and several other things that had taken our fancy.

Jack was keen to buy an alpenhorn and we eventually found a shop that had one and Jack bought it. It was about fifteen feet long but it could be taken apart in the middle. He strapped the two halves on top of the car for the drive home.

Halfway across France, he stopped the car and when Vera asked why, he said it was time he had a blow. With that he got out of the car and he assembled the alpenhorn and proceeded to blow it. It echoed all across the valley. Shortly after we drove on, a convoy of French Gendarmerie came towards us with blue lights flashing and sirens blaring. They went on past, but we thought perhaps Jack had caused a panic.

He told us never to joke with the Customs officers when we declared our souvenirs, as they took it seriously. When asked about his watch, Jack took it off.

He held it up, and he said, "Do you know how to use a watch as a compass."

The officer just looked without answering, and Jack said, "You just swing it around and around, and when you let go its gone west, so east is in the opposite direction."

After a pause the officer said, "I see sir."

When the officer saw the alpenhorn, he did not know what duty to charge as he'd never seen one. He was going to waive the duty until Jack started to explain about it. I was kicking him to let sleeping dogs lie, but to no avail. The officer then said that now he knew that it was a musical instrument he would have to look it up. I think that Jack finished up paying nearly as much as it had cost him.

We visited the village of Grindelwald, overlooked by the north face of the Eiger. It was a beautiful unspoilt village then, and we decided to return that winter for the skiing. None of us had skied before and we thought it would be of benefit to have lessons when we returned to England.

There was a ski shop in Bromley called Pindi-Sports, with a warehouse that had a dry ski slope. It was made out of stiff fibre matting, constructed on wooden planks, and built with scaffolding. At the bottom was a huge girder that was wrapped in straw.

Learning to snowplough, Jack lost control and he sped off down the slope. He planted his ski stick to try to stop but it went through a knothole. It jerked him backwards and as the wrist band snapped, Jack hit the scaffolding and carried on down. He hit the girder at the bottom and finished up in a tangled heap of straw and skis. We all laughed, and he just got up and climbed back up again.

***

Every year the BBC would broadcast a commentary on the Monte Carlo Rally. Raymond Baxter, an ex-Spitfire pilot would commentate as well as compete. His vivid accounts of the driving conditions that they had to tackle, and his description of driving through the dripping tunnels of the Col de Tende, gripped my imagination. The starting points were from different places in Europe and in Scandinavia, and the teams would link up for the final part, around Monte Carlo.

When the starters from Scotland were heading down for Dover, I'd follow them as they came through Kent. Paddy Hopkirk, Stirling Moss and his sister Pat would compete, as well as amateurs. I could not afford to enter but I longed to test my driving skills in those conditions.

The week before Christmas there was no racing, so I was free. I'd bought a Sunbeam sports saloon and I fitted it with a roof mounted spotlight, that Jill could operate from the passenger seat. Now at last I could achieve my ambition to experience the winter driving conditions in the Alps. I did not however fit winter tyres.

We caught the Saturday midnight boat to Dunkirk, and we landed at 4.30 a.m. The roads through northern France were covered in black ice and there was a freezing fog. I spun the car several times, but I managed to control the skids. By the time we reached Pontarlier there was heavy snow and we had to wait for the snow ploughs to clear the road.

These were huge machines that pushed the snow to each side, leaving it piled up ten feet high, with just a single car track through it.

The Jura mountain roads were all ice and snow and the windscreen kept steaming up from my hot breath. We did not arrive in Grindelwald until nine p.m. that night, but I had enjoyed every minute. Jill had some nervous moments but she had faith in me, and she never doubted my ability.

The next day it was bitterly cold, and in the shade of the Eiger, there was no sun in the village all day. We hired skis which were the long wooden types, and boots which were, attached to the skis with bindings with spring releases and leather straps.

We joined the ski school for lessons, and we were the only ones there, as it was not due to open until after Christmas. We caught the chairlift up to 'First', and the lift man wrapped us in Eskimo-like blankets, but in the shade we still felt cold. At the top, however, it was beautiful, and we enjoyed learning to ski in warm sunshine.

We stopped for lunch at a little mountain restaurant at 'Bort' that was run by a friendly, rotund old lady who cooked us ham, egg and chips.

We arrived back at the village in the afternoon and we went to a tearoom for patisseries, gateaux and schnapps.

I left on Christmas day, I drove back over the Alps and through the night to catch the first boat on Boxing day, and I was back in the office in time for the Boxing days racing.

Skiing had whetted my appetite and I never missed a winter's skiing for the next thirty years after that.

***

I covered tens of thousands of miles without an accident, except for three minor incidents. Once, an oncoming lorry almost forced me off the road, and I skidded and caught the rear wheel hub on a rock face.

On another occasion, when avoiding a tram in Neuchatel I skidded on the ice into the kerb and I caught the door handle on the metal upright of a bus shelter.

The third wasn't really an accident as one of my rear chains broke and flailed around the wheel arch before I could stop. It was compulsory in Switzerland to carry chains and to fit winter tyres. Of course, there were not seat belts or air bags then, so I guess I was lucky.

On narrow mountain roads on ice, Jill was sometimes a bit apprehensive, when we were only a few feet from the edge of a precipice.

***

We returned to the Hotel Krebs in Interlaken the following summer. The hotel concierge was Armin Berchtold who told us that he was a ski instructor in winter and that he had a chalet in Riederalp, and that he took in guests. He said why do we not go to him that winter as it was a high village at two thousand metres.

The village is accessible only by telepherique and it was guaranteed to have snow. It was at the end of the Aletsch Glacier, the longest glacier in the Swiss Alps.

It was a long drive from Lake Geneva to the end of the Rhone valley but well worth it. Jill and I went and we enjoyed skiing in brilliant winter sunshine on deep powder snow. There were no piste making machines then, and the runs were made by the lift men skiing down from the top, holding two wooden shafts with a roll of wire behind them.

The ski acrobat Art Furrer came from there. He spent much of his time in the States but when he was home on holiday, he would ski down from the top on one leg, with the other leg twisted up behind him and the ski above his head. I tried it and I could just manage it, but only on a gentle slope. He later opened an apartment block and a restaurant, and on later holidays we would often eat there. He ran the ski school and Jill and I took the Swiss Ski Test. She got the bronze medal and I managed the silver.

Jill and I were able to go to Switzerland mostly in winter for long periods every year, when National Hunt racing had virtually shut down. It was the Cinderella side of racing and there were no all-weather tracks and much fewer meetings than now. Anytime there was frost, snow, fog or rain they could not race.

The main income came from the flat race season, and the winter just ticked over with greyhound racing and football. I was able to leave Den to run things, but I always phoned him to let him know where I was, just in case I needed to return home for any emergency.

Silver City Airlines operated a car ferry service from Lydd in Kent. At first, they used converted Douglas Dakota aircraft, then later the Bristol Air Freighter. The nose of the plane was hinged, so that it opened for cars to be driven on. It only took a few cars and the drivers, and the passengers sat in a small cabin behind the pilot. Nevertheless, it had a duty-free cupboard and an air hostess to serve you.

Customs was a little shed, and when you arrived there were hardly any formalities. The flight only took about twenty-five minutes and you landed at Le Touquet and you could then drive off through France.

***

One winter, Jack and Vera came to Grindelwald, and Jill and I had ten days with them before we went on to Riederalp.

The village postmen would deliver the mail with the mail sack swung over their shoulders and pushing a ski bike. Not like those you see today, these were wooden, with a metal runner at the back and another at the front, attached to a pole and handlebars. They were made by a village craftsman. When the postman had delivered the mail to the chalets at the top of the mountain, he would get on the bike and ride back down on the icy paths.

Jill loved seeing them. I found the craftsman and I got him to make her one. There was not much snow and the roads were icy, so we all had a go on it.

Jack had come in his Jaguar E-Type. We had previously watched Ski Joëring in St Moritz. They race on the frozen lake with the skier behind a horse that has long reigns attached to it.

Jack suggested that I did this on the ski bike, being towed with a rope fixed to the handlebars and tied behind the E-Type.

Off we went up the mountain with Jill sitting beside him. When we got to the top, I untied the rope and I rode off down the icy paths to the village. Jill filmed it, and I still have the super eight cine film.

We stayed at the Hotel Oberland, a family hotel run by Peter Kaufman. It's been pulled down and developed now, but back then it was a typical old Swiss hotel. The family were very obliging, and the meals were excellent. When we left, I told Jack that I would pay, and that he could settle with me later.

The morning we left was very cold and icy. We had parked outside the hotel and Jack had covered his windscreen with a large sheet of plastic to prevent it being iced up. He took it off and laid it on the icy road in front of the car, ready to fold it up.

When he looked up, he saw Vera coming out of the hotel, carrying the case that held his Bolex cine camera. Thinking that she might slip and drop it; Jack went over and took it from her. Walking back to his car he stepped on the plastic, and as it slipped away Jack somersaulted over backwards. As he did, he threw the camera up in the air and it came down, hit the road, and slithered along it. A big lorry was coming, and the camera shot underneath missing all four wheels. It hit the kerb and continued sliding along the road.

When Jack recovered it, he was relieved to find that it was not damaged. I had seen the whole thing and could not stop laughing.

We said our goodbyes and the family waved us off. Jack was in front and I followed in my car.

Halfway to Interlaken I was talking to Jill about our stay and I remarked on how cheap it was. Calculating it in my head I then realized that Frau Kaufman had only charged me for one couple and not two.

Whenever we were travelling in separate cars, we had an arrangement that if the car behind needed to stop, he would flash the other one three times. I did this and I explained to Jack why we had stopped. We then drove back to the hotel. Frau Kaufman said that she had known that she had only charged for one couple but she did not want to tell me.

There were other times when this happened. On our way to Monaco one year, Jill and I stopped overnight at a small hotel in Brignoles on the Côte d'Azur. At dinner the patron tried to explain the menu to us. It was un liévre. We did not understand so he drew a picture on the tablecloth.

We said, "Ah, rabbit, la lapin."

He then added two long ears to the drawing, and we recognised it as a hare.

The next day we left, and Jill went to the co-op to get us something for a picnic lunch. I sat in the car and then I realised that he'd charged for the dinner and the wine but not for the room. We went back and we told him, and he was very surprised at our honesty.

Apart from Gran telling me that honesty was the best policy, I always felt that when I was abroad, that I was representing England.

On other occasions, when a waiter had undercharged me, I would call him, and I would say that the bill was wrong. He would apologise and take it away. When he came back to say that he'd checked it and he could not find anything wrong, he would then be astonished when I pointed out that he had not charged me enough. I still continue to do this unless the meal has been bad and the service poor.

***

I would drive around to all the main ski resorts to find the best snow, but we usually finished up at Riederalp.

One morning on the sunlit balcony, there was a French couple with their two children, and the mother was taking their photo. Jill asked if she could take it, so that they could all be in it together. They were also staying at Armin's, and after that we skied together and played cards in the evening.

The following year, we met up again quite by chance, and when they left, they invited us to visit them in Paris. The following Easter we did.

There was no racing on Good Friday and the week before it was a quiet one; so, we flew from Heathrow and they met us at Orly Airport. The plane was the French Caravelle, and from take-off, it climbed almost vertically to more than thirty thousand feet. The noise was deafening and there was so much vibration I thought that the wings would drop off.

Charlie and Franzi Tuerlinckx and their two children Mark and Barbara lived in Crosne, on the outskirts of Paris. Their house was a large château and in the grounds was a factory. They made reproduction furniture and office panelling.

Charlie was a typical Frenchman, tall with a large moustache, and he spoke little English. Franzi, on the other hand was Swiss, and she was fluent in several languages. As a teenager she had been an au pair in London.

They took us to all the interesting places and Mark, their teenage son, took us to the Louvre. I wanted to see the Mona Lisa, but he was puzzled until he realised, they call it the La Gioconda.

Charlie and Franzi took us to a restaurant on the Champs-Elysees called L'entrecôte one lunchtime. The menu was steak and pomme frite.

The restaurant was decorated with large mirrors and the waitresses wore short skirts and lace pinnies and they buzzed around like flies. The meal was delicious, and I've always remembered it.

In the evening we went to the Crazy Horse Cabaret. All the dancers were naked, and it was nothing like what I'd seen at the Windmill Theatre in London when I was a boy.

I had to return to London on Good Friday, but the workers at Orly went on strike. The only flight that we could get was first class from Charles de Gaulle Airport.

Franzi took us after lunch and we boarded the De Havilland Trident. We sat up front in a separate compartment with armchairs and a coffee table between us. When the air hostess came, I refused lunch as we'd already eaten. We had coffee and the cup handle slipped around my finger and shot the lot over the magazine rack.

Jill told me afterwards that the menu showed that they served champagne with the lunch we'd declined. They called the Trident the whispering giant, and it's the quietist and the smoothest aircraft that I've ever travelled in.

We stayed with them several times after that and Charlie always did all he could to beat me, whether it was at table tennis, when he would cheat over the score, or at skiing, where he'd try to push me off the lift if we went up together. It was always France versus England.

Charlie knew that I'd taken up clay pigeon shooting, so he took me to the Shooting Club of Paris. He hired a gun for me and we shot the Olympic Trap layout. These targets fly away at high speed and it is a difficult discipline.

We had loaders standing behind us. Charlie's score was not bad, but my hits were poor.

Every time I missed the loader would say, "Derriere monsieur."

Franzi asked Jill, "Why is Ray not hitting them?"

Jill did not know what to say so she said, "Well he doesn't have his glasses."

Knowing that I was left-handed, Charlie had hired me a gun with a stock cast for a right hander.

He bought a horse and he took up show jumping, and he thought that he would become the French champion.

One night he took us to his Paris riding club. Jill and Franzi sat in the gallery with the other guests.

Charlie jumped a good round with his horse and then it was my turn. He'd mounted me on a horse that had a habit of refusing.

It jumped well until we got to the last fence, where it refused. I circled and I approached it again, but it refused to take off. I was determined that I would not let Charlie beat me, so I drove the horse forwards for the third time.

As I approached the fence, I heard them shout from the gallery, "NO RAY!"

But I gave the horse a whack and drove it on. It did not hesitate and we sailed over. To give him his due, Charlie arranged for a wonderful dinner in the club restaurant.

We started with langoustine, followed by a large roast and of course plenty of French wine. On another evening, to repay them, I took them to dinner.

Georges Carpentier had been a famous French heavyweight boxer who had a restaurant in Paris. We all went there, and I do not remember the meal, except that Franzi and I started with oysters that came on a large silver tray piled up with many different kinds of seafood.

***

One November, we were driving towards Neuchatel and I noticed a tack shop. I stopped and I went in and bought some riding gloves. I asked the assistant if he knew of anywhere that horses could be hired. He suggested that I try in a village close bye called Finsterhennen. It was another 'Fickle Finger of Fate' moment.

In Finsterhennen there was a man named William Marolf. He'd begun as a pig farmer but he had built up an engineering business making farm machinery. He specialised in large farm trailers and these were painted green with W.M. painted on the sides in large letters.

His hobby was horses, and when he became wealthy, he built stables there, together with a very big indoor riding hall. He also built an apartment block. He had a horse called Marianka that he had taken to the Mexico Olympics with the Swiss Olympic Equestrian team. Arthur

Blickenstorfer was his rider and Bruno Grolf the Olympic trainer. We went there and we met Frau Marolf. She did not speak much English but she explained that we could stay, and riding could be arranged.

We took one of the apartments; we were the only ones staying there.

The next day it was arranged for us to have lessons with the Swiss trainer. The riding hall reminded me of Wembley stadium and I'd never seen such immaculate stables. The horses were large, as like the Germans, the Swiss favoured the bigger types, especially for jumping. The first one that I rode was a 18hh named Freddie.

Because of his height he made even the large fences look small. Both Jill and I took lessons, but Jill would finish earlier as she found it tiring.

Some days we would ride out. The first time that I was given a Russian horse he was sensitive in the mouth and when I collected up the reigns, he backed me all around the yard.

The horses were fitted with studded shoes because of the ice and it set up a hell of a clatter.

We rode out with Bruno Grolf, through the countryside where women were working in the fields harvesting leeks. It was bitterly cold, and they had thick shawls over their shoulders.

A partridge suddenly took off beside me and the Russian horse went frantic. I managed to get him back under control and we rode on.

Riding along beside a canal, we came to the road and we needed to use it to cross over the bridge. Just as we did, I could see a tanker lorry approaching from the opposite direction. I thought that I could finish up in the frozen canal if it spooked the horse, but it went past without incident.

When we got back the farm women were washing off the leeks in the trough. Their hands must have been frozen. Bruno Grolf, the trainer, asked my name. I told him that it was Ray Saunders and after that he called me Mr Ray.

I would ride in the hall with Art Blickenstorfer and Bruno would stand in the centre giving instructions. Sometimes he would ride alongside me and instruct me on the correct leg controls to use.

One day, mounted on a little (for the Swiss) black stallion called Sombrero, Bruno was teaching me high school dressage movements. The horse was the most supple and responsive animal that I had ever ridden.

When we finished, he said to Jill, "Mr Ray is very good."

Later, I found out that the horse was an Andalusian.

Famous riders such as the Italian brothers Raimondo and Piero D'Inzeo and the German Alwin Schockemöhle would go there, but Jill and I were the first English people to stay there. We continued to go every year. Art Blickenstorfer left six years later but Bruno Grolf stayed on.

Frau Marolf would often come and sit with us after dinner and she enjoyed trying to practise her English.

One night, after a waitress, who was obviously pregnant, had left, she tried to explain something to us. Finally, she took hold of the third finger of her left hand and she wiggled it while pulling a face.

Jill said, "She's telling us that the girl isn't married."

The Swiss do not celebrate Christmas as we do. They celebrate St. Nicholas day on the Sixth of December when they give presents. A donkey would go around the village with a man dressed as the saint, giving out gifts to the children. Frau Marolf proudly showed us a plastic mac that her granddaughter had given her. I remember thinking that here was a very wealthy woman who could still enjoy receiving a cheap item, because it had been given by a little child.

**

Years later, on a walking holiday, we called in to see them. They had both died and their son had taken over the business. All the horses were gone, and the riding hall was part of the factory and it was full of trailers.

Chapter 13

In 1964 the Wilson Government introduced travel restrictions and they limited the amount of money that you could take abroad. The maximum allowed was fifty pounds in travellers' cheques and twenty-five pounds in cash.

The exchange rate for Switzerland was very good at twelve Swiss francs to the pound, which made things relatively less expensive there, than they were in England. Even so it was difficult to budget on this.

I had a Triumph 2000 saloon and when a door was opened, there was an aluminium plate along the door sill, that covered the upturned weld. I found that by unscrewing the plate, five-pound notes could be inserted, and the plate fixed down again.

Jack Wells converted the large air filter on top of the E-Type's engine and he would pack notes inside it. When they were going through France, Vera would look in the driver's mirror, expecting to see them blowing out of the exhaust pipes. Changing them for Swiss currency in the banks was easy, but the notes needed a lot of straightening. Not knowing what the Swiss banks would do, we would go every morning and only exchange twenty-five pounds. After the third day the clerk told us that if we brought it all in at once, that he could give us a better rate of exchange.

***

Travelling through France, you were required to pay a room tax when you booked into a hotel for the night. You also had to fill in a form stating who you were. The Gendarmerie would come and check it every morning.

One night after a couple of bottles of wine, the concierge came to our table and he told us that we'd forgotten to fill in the forms. Jack and I signed as Harold Wilson and George Brown.

When they were checked the next day, we wondered what they would make of the Prime Minister of England and his Deputy, being on holiday together in France.

***

Jill and I were staying with Armin in Riederalp one time, when I realised, that I would not have enough money to pay the bill.

I rang Den and asked him to send me some money. I said that the best way was to roll it in a newspaper, as these were not checked.

I waited and nothing came, and as the time got nearer, I thought that I would not be able to pay. Every morning the locals would come in for their coffee and their schnapps and read the newspapers. These were kept on the shelf above the coat rack.

One morning Jill thought to look there, and sure enough there was one addressed to us that had been opened. She took it down and I looked through it but found nothing.

I said, "Somebody's had it, and that's the dearest bloody newspaper I shall ever buy."

Jill took it and looked through it carefully. Den had bought two identical local papers and cutting an advert out of one, he had then glued it around two fifty-pound notes in the other. What a relief and what an idea he'd had.

During a heavy snowfall one night, Armin knocked on our bedroom door. When I opened it, he was standing there in his nightshirt. He said that in the chalet below he could hear a woman screaming.

We opened our window, and below us there was a woman at her window and she shouted to Armin that someone had tried to strangle her. Armin said that we should go down. I got dressed and when I met Armin, he was wearing an army greatcoat and carrying an oil lamp and a rifle.

Every year all Swiss men, up to a certain age, have to do several weeks military training, and they take their rifles home with them. He said if I went in front with the lantern, he would follow behind with the gun.

I was not afraid of meeting the murderer, what concerned me the most was that if Armin slipped and pulled the trigger, he could shoot me.

When we got there, a great pile of snow had slipped off the roof when the assailant had jumped off the balcony to get away. Armin calmed her down and we left.

The next morning some detectives arrived from Brig and investigated. The woman's daughter admitted that she had arranged for a man to come to her after dark when her mother was asleep. He'd gone into the wrong room, and as he pulled the covers down in the dark, her mother had woken up thinking someone was about to strangle her. The detectives said that they were looking for a man who had not been home that night. When Armin went to take ski school later, none of the other ski instructors turned up.

***

One February, while we were in Switzerland, Den phoned me to say that Dusty was ill. I asked if it was serious and he said that he was not in hospital, but he had bronchial pneumonia. It sounded bad so we left immediately.

I drove all night and we reached Le Touquet and we caught the first flight.

When we arrived at their bungalow, Dusty was sitting in his armchair by the fire. He was still alive, but I could tell by the rattle of his breathing that he was dying. His eyes were closed, and I knelt beside him and I gripped his hand. I stayed like that until he slipped away. It was as though he had held on long enough for me to get there. He was almost eighty-eight.

Gran had always wanted a standard lamp. Two days before his death, Dusty had got up and he had walked to Tonbridge High Street and he bought one for her. He had carried it back all the way home. He'd always been an inspiration to me, and I loved him deeply. They'd been married for sixty-four years.

I'd always promised him that I would take care of Gran, so I set about her living with me. The tenants in my lower flat wanted a house. The council had an invalid couple living in a house, who needed a bungalow, so I arranged a three-way exchange and Gran moved in with us. Jill and I were still above in the top flat, and at night we could hear her snoring. If we could not hear anything I would go down and listen at her door to make sure that she was all right.

When we went down to Somerset, riding, we would take her with us. She loved it and she was always cheerful.

One night after dinner she said, "I've eaten so much my belly's so full I could crack a flea on it."

When we went off skiing, I arranged for meals on wheels for her. When we got back, she told us that she had cancelled them as they were like a lot of pap.

Den lived with his mother and his sister just across the road from us and he would pop in on her on his way to the office and again at night. If she wanted any shopping it was always a bunch of bananas and a pork chop.

Gran stayed with us for four years until she took ill and died in hospital shortly afterwards. She was also eighty-eight. They were both buried in Tonbridge cemetery, close to my mother.

***

There was a riding stables in Interlaken run by a man named Ernst Voegeli. His son was a captain in the Swiss cavalry, and we would hire horses and ride out with him. These rides could be quite adventurous.

The first day, as we went through a park, he jumped over all the benches with us following. We came to a hedge with a steep drop on the other side, he jumped it and I followed, but Jill did not want to.

He said, "Come, the horse will do it."

She was apprehensive but she did it.

The next morning, he said, "Today we ride in the lake."

Jill said to me, "I expect he means around the lake."

However, she was wrong. The lakes of Thun and Brienz join at Interlaken and it's just possible to ford them. Crossing them meant holding your legs up to the horse's neck, but we made it.

On another day we rode across an Air Force runway. The jets were lined up outside the hangers ready for take-off and I hoped that we'd be across before they did.

The captain told us that he was coming to England and did I know anyone at Lloyds of London. The film 'On Her Majesty's Secret Service' had been made there. The scenes had been shot on the Schilthorn above the village of Murren. The summit is 9744 feet. Piz Gloria is a panoramic revolving restaurant at the top.

Once, Jill with two friends and I, had gone there for lunch. The dessert was various ice creams and fruit, in a large glass dish and it was called a 007. When I saw the size, I ordered one and four spoons. We shared it, and I said that we'd each had a double 'O' one and three quarters.

The film was shot there and each day a helicopter would land and take the day's shooting to Geneva, to be flown back to England.

One scene involved an open landau that had been specially brought from Russia. Herr Voegeli had supplied two matching Hafflinger horses for the film.

As they were coming down the narrow track through the snow, the helicopter took off and the horses bolted. A Jeep from the film company was coming up and ran into them on a bend. It smashed the Russian landau and killed one horse.

The other horse was so badly injured that it had to be put down. Our captain was trying to claim compensation, but the film company was saying that it should be on the helicopter's insurance, and they said that it was the film-maker's responsibility.

I told him that I was sorry, but I knew of no one who could help him, and I wished him luck.

***

Every November it became my routine the drive down to Monaco and to spend ten days or so there, before driving back over the Alps to Switzerland.

We would stay at the Garni Hotel Miramar. It was on the eastern side of the harbour, and from our balcony, we looked across the harbour to Prince Rainier's castle, perched on the rock.

Monaco today bears no resemblance to how it was then. They had not begun the development, and when I watch the Monaco Grand Prix on TV, I cannot recognise it.

It was small and picturesque, and in November the temperature was mild and usually sunny. The Monaco Rowing Club was next door to the hotel, and on Sunday mornings we would sit on our balcony having breakfast and watch them rowing around the harbour.

One morning a French submarine tied up alongside the harbour below our balcony. We watched as the submariners loaded up with fresh fruit, vegetables and water. It was a real rust bucket and I thought not a good advert for the French navy.

Each evening it was necessary to leave your breakfast order for the following morning with the concierge. We used to dine out at one of the little restaurants around the harbour, and one night when we returned to the hotel, I thought that I'd practise my French. Speaking to the concierge I said that I'd like breakfast to be served in our room at neuf hours, meaning at nine a.m. He thought I was ordering nine eggs, (oeufs) for breakfast. Luckily Jill had taken French lessons at school and she was able to rectify it.

We would walk up to the castle and sit outside the cafe by the square, looking across to the gates with a sentry box each side. Having coffee, we would watch the changing of the guard.

The new guards, dressed like toy soldiers and with drummers in front, would march out and perform the guard changing ritual. It was like watching a child's fairy story. Just around the corner was the old village and the cathedral, with a statue of St. Nicholas. This was the 'Place St Nicholas' where Grace Kelly had married Prince Rainier.

There was a little artist's studio nearby, and one day Jill and I went in. The artist was Roger Marie Carre and one painting caught our eye. It was of the statue and the old street, with people sitting under coloured umbrellas outside a café. I bought it for Jill and the artist asked me to sign his patron's book. I signed it Ray Saunders, Pardlestone Barton, England on the page opposite to that of General Charles De Galle's signature.

Further around the rock was a zoo overlooking the sea. Jill filmed it and we thought it very cruel. One tiger continuously walked around his small cage, and an elephant on a small area of rock just stood there swinging its head from side to side.

Above the harbour was the casino and the opera house. Beneath the casino was an indoor heated swimming pool that opened onto a balcony overlooking the Mediterranean. For a fee you could swim there, and Jill and I would walk up carrying our swimsuits in our Sealink carrier bag, to purchase the ticket.

The swimming pool was in the shape of a scallop shell, with a moulding of the shell for the ceiling. On one side were sun loungers, and the other side had a long bar where you could climb out of the water and sit on a bar stool to enjoy a Martini.

We had a private shower room and a changing cubicle. Outside on the balcony we'd have lunch, and we'd often listen to some old shipping magnate telling his female companion that his wife did not understand him. I'd go for a massage and lie there, looking out on the blue Med, feeling like James Bond.

Some nights we would go to the opera house. On one occasion it was an Italian pianist named André Soldes. After the interval, he came and sat with a woman in front of us. He never stopped talking to her throughout the second half. In the end, I could not put up with it any longer. I could not speak Italian, so I rapped him on the shoulder, and when he turned around, I put my finger to my lips and I said, "SHUSH". This stopped him for a while but not for long. I said, "Bloody Italians."

On another night, it was an orchestra and they announced that they would play a new work from a new young composer. It was a fearful dirge.

The woman sitting next to Jill in an evening dress and diamonds started to shout. "Cock a doodle doo! Cock a doodle doo!"

Jill looked at me and said, "What is she doing?"
I said that I thought she was giving it the bird.

Opposite the casino was the Hotel de Paris and one night we went there for dinner. In the corner of the dining room a small orchestra played. There was a solo guitarist, and when he'd finished playing there was no applause. He was very good, and I felt it discourteous that the diners had not applauded him. I began clapping, and the other tables looked at me and then they started to clap as well.

During the interval, the conductor came over and he asked if they could play a request for us. We chose a selection from South Pacific. I cannot remember what the meal cost, but afterwards I ordered my usual brandy. The wine waiter came, and he offered us either Remy Martin, or their own special one hundred and fifty-year-old Napoleon Brandy from their cask in the cellar. Jill said that she'd like to try it, so we did, but I could not tell the difference, except for the price.

Before we left, he told me that they sometimes sold it to special customers. It was sixty pounds a bottle, which in those days was three or four times the average weekly wage, so I politely refused the offer.

Our favourite restaurant was La Chaumière in Monte Carlo, that overlooked the Principality of Monaco. It had a fantastic view from the deck. To my surprise it is still there, and it can be found on the internet. It's changed somewhat but it still has the same wonderful view. Sunday lunch was very popular with the Monègasques and it was necessary to book.

It was our first time there and we thought the food was superb, and the service, with the owner's individual attention, made you feel special.

I remember how astonished we were when the chef came in with a basket of flowers and he showed us how he'd sculptured everyone from dyed potatoes. They looked so real we could hardly believe it. Even the basket looked like a plaited wicker basket but it was made from pastry.

One evening we went up to dinner and we were the only ones there. The owner apologised that the place was empty, but the chef cooked us a delicious meal. Afterwards, the owner came and sat with us and he bought us brandies.

Nearby was the 'Jardin Exotique de Monaco', built on a near vertical rock face. It was full of exotic plants. I have a cine film of Jill in her red leather suit, standing beneath an archway that has a magnificent red bougainvillea in full bloom, climbing over it. The garden is still there today, and the photos of it on the internet, are well worth a look.

Nearby is Grasse, known as the perfume factory of the world. Chanel No. 5 is made there. When we visited the factory, the chemists helped Jill to create her own perfume. Nearby are the cliff edge villages of Eze and Roquebrune where we watched an artisan making wooden objects.

He made Jill a large cheeseboard from olive wood, complete with handle and sculptured hollows for olives.

Alfred Hitchcock made a film called 'To Catch a Thief' that was filmed all around that area. It stars Cary Grant and Grace Kelly. When I watch the shots of them driving around the Riviera, along the Corniche, it brings back fond memories of how it was then. It also reminds me of the boy who, living in poverty, dreamed that one day he'd be able to do this.

***

After Gran died, I set about converting the two flats back into a proper house. I ripped out the old Victorian fireplaces, installed gas central heating and I created a 27x15 feet dining room. I made a built-in bar along one side and our dining table could seat twelve guests.

On removing the old lathe and plaster walls I found it slow work, so I bought a chain saw to speed things up by cutting them out. I'd already finished the front lounge and I had it fitted with wall to wall carpet. It was a beautiful woollen Axminster in a dark green Aztec design. One day as I was sawing away, Jill came to me in tears. She told me to stop as I'd ruined her lovely carpet.

When I looked, the fine plaster dust had completely covered the carpet in a white blanket. I told her not to step on it and I sent her to fetch the vacuum cleaner.

Starting at the door I worked my way across with the vacuum and I sucked it up. As the carpet was new and it had a woollen pile, the dust had only settled lightly on top. When I finished there was not a trace of it left. However, I did not use the chain saw on the plaster again.

When I had finished, I filled a large sack with the old plaster to take to the dump. At the back of the house there was a piece of land where I'd erected an old garage. Behind it was a small piece of concrete that met up with next door's garden. Not wishing to carry the heavy sack down and around to the garage, I opened the bathroom window and I lifted the sack onto the window ledge. It was three stories high on this side, and I looked down to see that it was all clear.

Shouting, "Geronimo!" I launched the sack off the ledge.

Just as I did, Mrs Wicket from next door appeared below, sweeping her garden path. The sack hit the ground and exploded like an atomic bomb. The cloud of dust completely engulfed her, and I thought that I might have given her a heart attack. I went to see if she was all right, but she was only shaken-up, so the next day I bought her a bunch of flowers.

There was a firm in Dover that made mahogany double-glazing units. The glass revolved so that it could be cleaned from the inside. I got them to replace all my old Victorian sash cord windows.

When they turned up, I could tell by their attitude, that the fitters were a load of cowboys. The job was not going to my liking, and one day I went into the dining room and one of the fitters was sitting smoking. He had removed the old window and he was sitting on the window ledge, kicking his heels against my newly decorated wall.

I pulled him off and I bundled him out the front door, and then I told the others to get into the van and leave. I rang the firm and I told them to deliver the rest of the windows and I fitted them myself.

During the war, the railings and the iron gates in houses were confiscated and they were taken to make munitions. There was a low brick boundary wall around my house with two brick pillars at the front where the gate had been. I went to a local firm called 'Hyders' in Plaxtol that specialised in wrought iron work and I had them make me gates and railings in wrought iron with roses in gold leaf. They did an excellent job and the old house finished up looking grand.

***

Exmoor continued to be my favourite place for riding, and in the village of Exford there's a hotel called 'The White Horse'. Next to it was a cottage and stables owned by Mrs Shedden. Her husband John was a leading equestrian rider and they kept some horses there for hunting. When they were not hunting, these horses could be hired. Their groom was Frank Mullins, an old-time horse master.

Jill and I would stay at the hotel and hire them. They told us at the hotel that Frank was a hard taskmaster and that he did not take kindly to anyone who did not treat his horses with respect. He was particularly abrasive with the hooray henry types who galloped his horses into the ground. They said that people found it hard to get along with him.

We hit it off from the start, and after riding, we would sit in the bar with him, buy him a pint, and he would talk about horse keeping. He taught me a lot which was to prove useful later. The barmaid was Eileen Ayliffe and she told us that her husband Nick had applied for a National Hunt trainer's licence. I still drank Remy Martin brandy, and she used to call me Mr Martin.

One night there was a father and son in the bar who were 'something in the city'. We got into a conversation and after more drinks they started to brag about how they had avoided the regulations and they were importing South African Kruger Rands, and they would then make a profit on the gold. When the conversation came around to me, they asked me what I did for a living and I told them that I was with Customs and Excise. They quickly drank up and left early the next morning.

Chapter 14

As a bookmaker I did not bet, but I started to play the stock market. My broker's name was Edwards, and my first shares were John Bloom the washing machine entrepreneur. My investment was a hundred pounds, and I lost it when he went into liquidation. It did not dissuade me though and I continued to invest, and at one time I had a considerable holding.

Mr Edwards invited Jill and I to the stock market and we looked over the dealings room, and then he took us to lunch. He gave us advice and I invested heavily in Rolls Royce and also BMC shares. Rolls shares had been dropping and I bought in at nineteen shillings.

I also bought William Hill shares. These had fallen because their profits were down, but I continued to buy them. I knew that their racing section was doing very well, and that it was the fixed odds war between them and Ladbrokes that was causing their losses.

I thought that this could not go on, and when Chancellor Reginald Maudling introduced a twenty-five percent betting tax on fixed odds betting, it finished it. Free of this burden, the shares went up. William Hill was against cash betting and he was reluctant to open betting shops. He finally had to give in and this addition to his empire once more caused the shares to skyrocket.

Returning from Switzerland one February, I heard on the car radio that Rolls Royce had been declared bankrupt. When I got home, I phoned my broker who told me that he'd been trying to contact me as I was one of his biggest holders. He said that the shares had stopped trading, but if I wanted to get out, that he could get me 2/6d a share from Canada.

Edward Heath was Prime Minister and I did not think that his government could possibly let a blue-chip company like Rolls Royce go under, so I said that I'd hang on with them. Heath took no action and I lost the whole holding.

***

Although cash betting had been legalised and it was now widely accepted, there were still certain regulations put in place. In order to control it, the government had included certain provisions in the Act. One of these was that although you could advertise your credit facilities, you were not allowed to advertise the cash side of the business.

I had fifteen thousand leaflets delivered in the area, stating that I was offering better odds and a better service, and I included my address.

One evening, while we entertained friends to dinner, the front doorbell rang. I answered it and a young police officer asked if he could come in. He then read out that anything I said would be taken down and used in evidence. He produced a leaflet that had been delivered to his house and he said that he was charging me.

I told him, "No comment," and he left.

Soon afterwards I was summoned to Tonbridge Magistrate's court and I was charged with a breach of the regulations.

On the day of the hearing I donned my Artillery tie and I went down to defend myself. I had prepared my case with adverts that I'd cut out of national newspapers, where all the leading bookmakers advertised their addresses and phone numbers. Of course, this was for credit betting and it did not breach the regulations. However, I calculated that the local magistrates might not be aware of the difference.

I took the stand and put it to them that if the big bookmakers could advertise their business, then surely it was only right that I should be able to do the same. I sat next to the police solicitor in court.

When they adjourned, he said to me, "You've got this."

When they came back, they found me not guilty.

Shortly afterwards, I received the following telegram:

'POLICE COMMISIONER GEBBLES V YOURSELF IS DUE FOR HEARING MONDAY 20TH APRIL IN THE LORD CHIEF JUSTICE'S COURT, ROYAL COURTS OF JUSTICE, STRAND WC2 CROWN OFFICE'.

I rang my solicitor for his advice, and he told me that he could not defend me as it had to be a barrister. I asked how much it would cost, and it was staggering. I said that I could not afford that, and he said that the only other thing was to defend myself. I had not been aware of this, and the thought exited me.

Poor Jill though, had sleepless nights before the trial.

On the day of the trial I dressed in my dark 'court suit' and of course my regimental artillery tie.

Reaching the court, I went up the entrance steps with my briefcase and carrying a rolled umbrella. Jill came with me and we were met by the usher.

When I showed him my summons, he said, "You've got the governor's court number one." He then added, "Well you're wearing the right tie."

He showed me to the door and on it was a notice that read:
'THE LORD CHIEF JUSTICE OF ENGLAND LORD PARKER. MR. JUSTICE BRIDGE, MR. JUSTICE BEAN'.

I went in and I found a seat at the front, and Jill went up into the spectator's gallery.

As I sat there, a barrister in his gown and wig came down and asked me if I was sitting there, and I said yes. He said that he always sat there, and what firm was I with. I said that I was not with a firm; I was defending myself. With that he sat somewhere else.

We all rose when the judges came in wearing their robes and their long wigs. The Lord Chief Justice sat in the middle, with the other two judges on either side. Looking up to them was quite daunting, but I did not feel at all nervous. There was one case before mine. The barrister defending the case kept bumbling, and the Lord Chief Justice castigated him for his incompetence.

All he kept saying was, "I apologise M' Lud."

Lord Parker was the last of the hanging judges, who would don a black cap and pronounce the death sentence. I was glad that mine was only a civil case.

My turn came and I said my piece. Anything I said that was not allowed, the Lord Chief Justice informed me and he showed me great tolerance as a layman. He heard the police barrister, Mr Lewis, put their case, and then it was time for the summing up. He told me about the law, and he said that not only had I given my address; I had also stated that there was a car park nearby.

He said that he was afraid that he would have to rule against me. The other two judges agreed. With that the police barrister stood up and he asked for costs.

The following is part of the court transcript that was sent to me later:

THE LORD CHIEF JUSTICE: They are asking you to pay the costs here today. It is difficult for you to oppose that.

THE RESPONDENT: I do not know. It seems to me that this appeal is taking place because the Magistrates have failed to convict me in the first place. It is their mistake and not mine.

THE LORD CHIEF JUSTICE: You are persuasive; you persuaded them.

THE RESPONDENT: No, I simply put the facts as I saw them, and I put forward the evidence that I have here, and if they judged wrongly I feel it is their responsibility and hardly mine, if I had to come along here today and go through this again. I would have thought that they are not entitled to costs.

THE LORD CHIEF JUSTICE: Mr. Lewis, this is no way a test case is it?

MR LEWIS: No, my Lord, not as I'm instructed.

THE LORD CHIEF JUSTICE: We are told that similar advertisements have been issued. Is this to try and see what the true position is?

MR LEWIS: My instructions are that certainly in the County of Kent this advertisement has never come to the notice of the authorities hitherto.

MR JUSTICE BRIDGE: It is a little hard, Mr Lewis, is it not?

THE LORD CHIEF JUSTICE: You might take further instructions and mention it at two o'clock, unless you can take them at once.

MR LEWIS: My Lord, I do not persist in my application.

THE LORD CHIEF JUSTICE: We have done something for you Mr Saunders.

THE RESPONDENT Thank you, my Lord.

THE LORD CHIEF JUSTICE: No order as to costs.

THE RESPONDENT: Thank you, my Lord, I'm obliged.

When he had said to the police barrister that he would have to come back at two o'clock, the Lord Chief Justice looked at the clock, and I could see by his face that he did not want to. He had saved me a lot of money and I felt that he was sympathetic towards me. I felt that I'd had a moral victory.

Jill was relieved and we celebrated by having a nice dinner, and afterwards going to the theatre to see Alastair Sim in a West End comedy play called 'The Magistrate'.

Later that month, I returned to the Tonbridge court where I was fined five pounds.

I could not help thinking how lucky I was to be living in a country where any individual, even one brought up in poverty, can defend himself in the highest court in the land, before the very top judge of the justice system. I had thoroughly enjoyed the whole thing and I would not have missed it for the world. After it was over, Jill was very relieved.

***

The following year Jill began to feel uncomfortable in her stomach. Swimming seemed the only thing that gave her relief. Doctor Forsythe had been their family doctor for many years, so we went to see him. He examined her and he said that he thought it was a growth. She had some tests and he then arranged for a consultation with a gynaecologist. This was Mr. Gordon Hill and we went to his private consulting room at his home in Tunbridge Wells. He examined her and he said that it was a large fibroid. I said that there was no lump, and he took my hand and he placed it on her stomach. I told him that I could not feel anything except that her stomach felt hard.

He said, "That's it. It's as big as a football."

I asked if it could be cancerous, and he replied that they rarely were, but that he could not be certain until he operated. He booked her in at the Nuffield Hospital for the operation and he said that it would be a full hysterectomy.

Jill was only thirty-eight, and he said that this would mean that she would not be able to have children.

When Jill and I had married we had discussed having a family, but she was not keen, and I had a lot of catching up to do and I was not keen either, as it would hold me back. We agreed that if either one of us changed our mind that we would then have children. We never did, so it wasn't a problem.

On the day of the operation I took her in, and Gordon Hill met us, and he introduced us to the anaesthetist. He said that he'd phone me when he'd performed the operation.

I went back to the office, but he did not phone, so I finished work and I went home.

I could not eat or settle down and I just stood looking out of the window. I kept remembering how horribly my mother had died from cancer and the thought haunted me. I did not know if there was such a thing as telepathy, but I tried to picture her being operated on, and I willed all my strength to her until I felt drained.

The phone rang and a voice said, "Mr Saunders, this is Mr. Hill's secretary, he'd like to speak to you."

Her voice was low and mournful, and I knew that my worst fears were true. My heart and my insides hit the floor and I felt devastated.

The next moment, I heard him say, "Hello Mr Saunders, the operation went well and Jill is recovering nicely, and there are no complications."

Never in all my life have I felt more relieved or elated. We later took him and the anaesthetist and their wives out to dinner. Gordon ordered partridge, and when it came, I was amused to see him operate on it.

I felt that we'd been given a reprieve and another chance at life together, and I was going to make the most of it. I wanted to have my own horses, and on our visits to Exmoor, I began looking for a suitable place.

A cottage next to our friends, the Lamacraft's, was coming up for auction. It would be ideal as I could then have the horses at livery at their stables. On the day of the auction, I drove down intending to buy it.

On the way, I pulled into a lay-by and we sat drinking a flask of coffee. The next minute, a van pulled in but it did not stop and it smashed into my boot. The damage was considerable and although the car was just drivable, Jill wanted to go back home., I would have in any case been too late for the auction It was another 'Fickle Finger of Fate' moment for had I bought the cottage the whole direction of my life after that would have altered.

We went to Switzerland that winter and when we returned, there was a letter from Dorothy Lamacraft, Edgar's wife. She had previously bought a partly converted barn on the Quantock Hills in Somerset and she rented it to her cousin.

He was a head teacher who had returned from Bermuda because of the troubles, but his wife missed the life and having servants, so they had not stayed long before going back.

She offered it to me as she wanted to pay off the mortgage. She asked if I would be interested in buying it before it went on the market. I had driven past the Quantocks many times but I did not know anything about the area.

For some time, I'd been thinking of selling up my share holdings, as I thought that a crash was coming, so this would be the opportunity.

We arranged to meet up there, and they would show me the surrounding area.

It was a mile up a winding, narrow lane on the north side of the hills. As we drove into the driveway, I saw this big old barn with a small dwelling built on one end, and a derelict outline of a building at the other. Opposite was a row of stables that were in poor condition and had been used to keep chickens. It was three acres in all, with an orchard that could hardly be seen through for brambles. There were tall nettles everywhere, and at the derelict end the whole area was a manure heap.

I fell in love with it immediately, as I could see at once the potential that it had. Jill agreed and I said that I'd buy it.

Dorothy was a shrewd businesswoman, and in the following weeks she kept asking for more as she had seen my enthusiasm. I made her my final offer and she accepted.

We arranged that Jill, her mother and her father would go and live there, and I would commute to and from Tonbridge. Len was retired and he loved gardening. He and Jill began clearing the ground. Den would have Mondays off so I would drive down on Monday night after racing and spend the week working on the stables. I'd then drive back on Friday night so that I would be there for Saturday's racing.

I applied for planning permission, which was granted, and I had the derelict end made into a self-contained annexe. I had a chap with a bulldozer to reshape the sloping terrain and I had the drive gravelled that had previously been mud. There was a tremendous amount of work to do before I could think about having horses there. I estimated that it would take me three years, but it took me five.

Len had been a driver all his life, but he had never owned his own car. His favourite make was Vauxhall. One day when I called into my local garage, there was a second-hand Vauxhall VX90 saloon with twin carburetors. It was painted in two-tone red and grey, with an all red interior.

I told Jill, and I said that I'd like to buy it for him.

I drove it home and I showed it to him, and I said what did he think of my new car.

He loved it and then I said, "Well it's not mine, it's yours."

At first, he could not believe it and then when he realised that I wasn't joking, his face lit up. He spent hours polishing it and I never saw it dirty. Len was a simple man, not meaning in intelligence. He was happy with the simple things in life and he was never happier than when he worked in the garden or helping me. He and Jill had planted a vegetable garden and I planted a small vineyard.

It took several years to produce enough grapes to make wine, but when it did, I made a hundred and fifty bottles.

In the following years, we would have friends and family come to us at grape harvest time and we would have great fun, with me treading the grapes. We would set up tables and chairs by the barn and have barbecues and barn dances, when the previous year's vintage would be consumed.

Jill also made apple and elderflower wine. One year, the apple wine was dry, but the elderflower was too sweet. I mixed the two, to make them better and I bottled it. After a while, it blew the corks off as a second fermentation had taken place. I had inadvertently made champagne.

The property was in Pardlestone Lane and it was called Pardlestone Barton, being the name given to barns.

We named our sparkling wine 'Champardle'. Many bottles were consumed when we had parties with our neighbours. There was a TV programme called 'The Good Life' where a young couple had left their jobs to become self-sufficient, so we were nicknamed 'The Goods'.

Chapter 15

My dream of having my own horses was soon to be realised. I had never forgotten the black stallion that I'd ridden in Finsterhennen.

One day, I picked up a magazine and I saw an article called 'The Dancing Horses of Spain'. It was written by Neil Dougall who himself had spent many years in Spain.

As a young man coming from Australia, he had joined a man who ran a business exporting Spanish horses to Mexico. Neil knew all the studs and the whole setup. Under General Franco's rule, the military ran the breeding and they kept the stud register. No stallions could be exported.

After his death in 1975, two things happened. The export ban was lifted, and under the new democracy, the wealthy stud owners could no longer set their horses off against tax.

I contacted the magazine and they put me in touch with Neil, and I asked him if he could help me buy a pure-bred Spanish stallion. He said that he had not been in Spain for ten years, but that he would get in touch with his contacts there and see what was available. He phoned me to say that Paco Montano who was an agricultural scientist and stud adviser, knew that the leading stud of the Marquis of Salvatierra was reducing its breeding activities. I agreed to his fee to accompany me to buy a stallion, and he arranged for me to visit the Finca Mahaloba near Seville.

I was in Kent covering the business, and I rang Jill to tell her that I was going to Spain to buy a stallion.

She said, "What about me?"

I thought she meant that she would like one as well, so I rang Neil back and I said that I wanted two. She had only meant what about her going to Spain with me.

There were restrictions on exporting money abroad and it could only be done if you provided a bill of sale. I could not do this, as I had to see the stallions first, and I then needed the money there to clinch the deal.

My neighbour in Somerset was Jeff Nash who was the manager of a local bank. He arranged with Lloyds International in Bristol to get me permission for a money transfer to the Banco Popular in Seville.

Iberian Airways had no direct flights to Seville and we had to connect with another flight at Valencia. It was pitch black and raining when we landed, and we transferred to a flight to Seville. I do not know what type of plane it was; I only remember that it had to be boarded by a ladder under the fuselage.

When I looked at the engines, they were covered in black oil stains. When we landed, I went to the Avis office for the car that we had booked. I had obtained my international drivers' licence, as was necessary then, and with Jill and Neil, I drove off into the night to find the Hotel Alcazar.

The next day, we drove to the stud to see what was on offer. Paco was there and I was shown four stallions. I examined them and I decided on the two that I would buy, and it was arranged for me to meet the Marquis the next morning at his office in Seville.

I do not speak Spanish, but Neil was fluent, and he did all the translations.

It was lunchtime and Neil had spotted a cantina at the end of the lane, so I drove us there.

Pulling up outside, we saw that it was closed, and we were about to leave when a car drew in behind us. Neil went to ask the driver if there was another cantina nearby that would be open.

It turned out that this man, Señor La Lune, was a builder who had a horse liveried at the Finca, and he had been there watching me as I examined the stallions.

Neil told me that he had said that he thought that I knew a lot about horses and that he would like to discuss them with me. He said I should follow him to Seville where he knew of a restaurant. I did, and in Seville I had to make sure I that did not get left at the traffic lights, as I did not have a clue where he was taking us.

When we arrived, we went inside, and Neil translated while we stood at the bar drinking 'La Ina' and eating a selection of tapas. They were delicious and the barman kept bringing them and he kept tally by chalking it down on the counter.

I thought that this was our lunch but 'Mr Moon' (La Lune) took us upstairs to the restaurant where we had more wine and a giant paella. When I told Neil to get the bill, he said that our host had an account there and that lunch was on him.

When we left, he told me to follow him and that he would guide us to our hotel. He sped off with me in hot pursuit, when suddenly the car swerved violently. Neil asked what the matter was, and I told him that we had a puncture.

I stopped, but 'Mr Moon' had carried on. I was about to open the boot for the jack, when he appeared again, reversing though the traffic lights, to pull up beside us. He insisted that he change the wheel for me, and afterwards we followed him again. When we reached our hotel, he just waved to us and disappeared. I never saw him again, but I remember his generosity and his good will towards us. He fascinated Jill with his dark brown eyes and his long eyelashes.

The next day we returned to the stud farm as I wanted to ride the horses before clinching the deal. I rode Jubiloso, and the *mayoral* (stud manager) rode Ganador. Neil was mounted on an older stallion, but Jill was on a gelding, as the Spanish were very macho then, and they thought a woman should not ride a stallion.

No sooner had we started than Jubiloso begun bucking. Neil thought that this would put me off, but I told him that it showed that the horse had spirit. The horses had only been broken to saddle recently, and they had been part of the team who won the Spanish National Driving Championships.

We rode out through the countryside and through cotton fields where the women were working picking cotton. It reminded me of the old films of the American deep south, with the cotton plantations.

When we got back, the *mayoral* put them both in harness and he drove Jill around the orange groves in an open landau. She picked a Seville orange and I still have it in a little glass dish on the window ledge. It has shrivelled to the size of a golf ball but is still recognisable.

***

Neil had been friendly with John Fulton, the American painter and bullfighter, who had a studio there. Neil got in touch and we visited his studio and we bought two of his paintings. He invited us to dinner, and he arranged to pick us up at ten p.m. that night. When he turned up, he had Robert Vavra the photographer with him. They had an apartment there that was being renovated.

The restaurant was an old-fashioned place and we had to go through the kitchen to get to the dining room. We sat at a round table that had a supporting pole in the middle, attached to the ceiling. After the meal, they insisted that we all go back to their apartment.

When we arrived, there was chaos everywhere with cables and fittings. John said that there was not enough room in the bathroom for a full-sized bath and they wanted to install a sit-up type bath. He said that no way would he have that, so, a full-sized bath was installed, with the end poking out through the wall onto the patio.

John Fulton was one of only two Americans to obtain full Spanish matador status. Apart from his artistic business he exported matador costumes to Mexico. He had a consignment packed ready for shipping, but he wanted us to see them first. I was amazed at their brilliance when he unpacked them. Thousands of sequins had been sewn onto them and he said that it took many hours for the women workers to do this by hand. He finally drove us back to our hotel.

When he left it was one thirty a.m. and we could hear music coming from a bar nearby. Neil said that he would like to treat me and Jill to a drink and to sample real Spanish night life.

It was Pepe's Bar and the music came from the cellar below. We went down and there were tables and chairs in a series of brick archways. The local young couples sat around with the boys playing guitars. We sat at a table and Neil ordered more bottles of La Ina. For those who do not know, this is a sherry type dry white wine.

In Seville, we had seen posters of a show with two dancers whose photos were displayed. As we sat there, two women accompanied by three or four male companions came down. One was a dark Spanish beauty and the other was Eurasian. Both wore stunning outfits and they were instantly recognisable as the two dancers.

After a while, the young guitarists struck up a tune and the dancers went up onto the small stage and performed a Flamenco, with castanets and much clapping. We finally left at four a.m.

The next day, Jill said that she had enjoyed it, except for the dense cigarette smoke. I said that I had not noticed it.

Later that day, Neil went with us to the office of the young Marquis and I discussed a deal with him. I said that I thought he was asking too much and if he was prepared to come down, as I was buying two stallions from Spain, and I had not yet been to another stud.

As he wanted them both to come from his stud, he agreed to this. I also arranged for him to keep them at livery until I could arrange for their transportation to England. We then went off to the bank to arrange payment. It was also necessary to obtain veterinary certificates in three languages, as they would have to go through France to reach the channel port.

We went to the British Consulate, and the Vice-Consul Carlos Formby, agreed to do that for me. Neil had to return home, and Jill and I stayed on for a few days.

I invited John Fulton and Robert Vavra, together with Paco Montana and his wife to dinner on our final night. Before we went to the restaurant, Paco took us to a new shop he and his wife were opening in Seville for veterinarian products.

The next day, we flew home, having had a very enjoyable trip. We had bought Robert Vavra's books showing wonderful photos of the Spanish horses, and the wild horses of the Camargue. We also had three sombreros, one for each of us and one for Jill's father.

***

It took me two months before I could arrange transport for the horses, but I eventually found an agent who had arranged for a horsebox to take a mare and a foal to Madrid, and I paid for them to continue down to pick up my stallions. This was early January and when they reached Cherbourg there was a gale in the channel and the horses weren't allowed to travel at anything above force six. The French customs had already delayed them at the Spanish border for thirty-six hours and they had started to run out of horse food.

They eventually crossed to Portsmouth and they arrived in Pardlestone at midnight, after four days travelling. The stallions had stood all that time and they had not been out of the horsebox for any exercise, as the young couple in charge were frightened of losing them.

***

Jill and I had two boxes ready and we offered the stallions food which they refused but they drank copiously. They then quickly laid down on the straw bedding and slept. It was obvious that they were exhausted, and their heads were going to and fro as if they were still travelling.

We sat up with them all night and in the morning, we were delighted to see that they had fully recovered. Our hay was a problem, as in Spain they are fed on alfalfa which is much courser. I bought an old chaff cutter and we chopped straw and mixed it with the hay, which they ate.

My next task was to obtain a stallion licence, as imported stallions had to be gelded if they did not pass a conformation test, and to make sure that they were also free of any diseases. A Ministry Vet came down from Reading to do the examinations and to my relief, he passed them both.

Jill and I then rode them both out together for two hours every morning on the Quantocks. After a while, I received a telephone call from a reporter, who had heard about us and he wanted to know about them.

The next thing there was a newspaper report about my adventure, saying that I was the first Englishman since Charles II to import Pure Bred Andalusian Stallions to this country.

***

That winter we had a terrific snowfall; the weight of which caused the rear of my stables to collapse. It meant that I had to livery the stallions with my friend John Lamacraft, while I fixed the damage. Considering that they had come from Spain; I was surprised to see how well they coped with our winter. Every time I led them out into the snow they got down and rolled and thoroughly enjoyed it.

The following spring John told me that the secretary of The British Association of Riding Schools was arranging to take a few owners to Andalusia to visit the studs there. He asked whether Jill and I would like to join them. We agreed and we all met up at Heathrow.

Several of the staff there knew John as they came down to his riding school for holidays. When we walked into the departure hall, with John carrying his old suitcase tied up with baler twine, there came an announcement, saying, 'Would Mr John Lamacraft and his party please go to reception in the VIP lounge'.

On the same holiday were a couple from Surrey, Bernard and Margaret Elliott. Bernard was a good rider, as was Margaret who had her own horse. We got on well and we toured the studs together.

John had been at Taunton school with the British Consul, who threw a cocktail party for us at the Consulate. We had spent the day visiting the equestrian school of Don Rafael Durando who, together with his daughter, gave a display of Spanish horsemanship. The girl groom, Brenda, was from Australia and John invited them all to the cocktail party that evening. Brenda had too much to drink and she offended the Consul's wife by coming on to him.

When it was time to leave, we had taxis outside waiting to take some of us on to a restaurant. Once outside, Brenda started to become noisy, so I bundled her into the back of a taxi with Bernard and Margaret. He told me later that within minutes she had tried to get his trousers off.

The next day, Jill told me that at the stud she had felt sorry for her, as she was lonely, and that she was going to return to Australia. She was breaking the journey with a few days in England and Jill had invited her to come and stay with us. Luckily, Brenda phoned us when she arrived in London to say that she could not make it.

***

Jill began to suffer with a back problem that was aggravated by riding. I was still commuting to and from Kent, but the business was in decline.

The Tonbridge office was suffering as Ladbrokes and Coral had moved into the town and there was now fierce competition.

It was obvious that I had to decide as to our future. The Paddock Wood office was still only opening part time and one option was for me to go back and live in our Tonbridge house and work full time there. This meant that I would be away from Pardlestone, and Jill would have difficulty coping on her own. I was however determined to pursue my life with her and the stallions, so I decided on a course of action.

I offered Den a full partnership in the business and I decided to close the Tonbridge office. We would then concentrate on the Paddock Wood office full-time. I installed the latest technology with several monitors displaying each afternoon's racing. Den agreed to run it, with the help of several part-time employees.

I would still cover his holidays and his sick leave, and of course Grand National day. I was then able to spend most of the year at Pardlestone with Jill.

We still enjoyed riding out together, but it was not long before she had to give up riding. Her stallion was Ganador who was a real character. I had taught both horses to urinate in a bucket for me. I would walk into their stable and whistle, I would hold the bucket underneath them, and they would duly oblige. This saved a lot of wet bedding.

We had started letting the annexe for holidays, and Jill's cousin Pat and her husband Jim from London, came to stay for a week.

One day Jim came to watch me as I walked into Jubiloso's box. When I held the bucket and I started to whistle, Jim asked me what I was doing. I told him that the horse would pee in the bucket. He watched in amazement.

As I walked into Ganador's box there was already a bucket with a hand shovel in it, just inside the door. Ganador went over to it and he picked up the shovel in his teeth and he walked around with it.

Jim said, "What is he doing Ray?"

I said, "Oh he picks up his own droppings."

Jim called to his wife, "Pat, Pat, come and see this you'll never believe it!"

We all had a good laugh when he realised, that I was just kidding him.

Jill finally gave up riding, so that she could concentrate on the garden with her father, growing vegetables. I now rode both stallions at exercise for four hours a day. This proved too much for me, so I sold Ganador. I kept Jubiloso as his conformation was better, and he would be better suited for breeding. Ganador went to a good home with a woman who lived in Yorkshire.

One night, Eileen, who we had met at the White Horse, came to dinner with her husband Nick, who had just been granted his trainer's licence. During dinner he asked Jill if she would like to buy a half share in one of his National Hunt horses. Jill was quite excited to become a racehorse owner, so it was agreed. It would run in her colours, so she chose a design and her silks were made up.

The horse was a mare called Flaxen Forest but before it was due to run it was found to be in foal. Nick said not to worry, as he could find another one. The second horse was Charig's Company and we went to several racecourses in England and Wales to watch it run. Jill's jockey was Philip Hobbs who is now a leading trainer.

The horse was always disappointing, but on one very cold day at Worcester, it was challenging the odds-on favourite, when to Jill's dismay, it suddenly pulled up. It had broken a blood vessel which affects a horse's breathing.

By this time Jill was becoming fed up with writing cheques out to Wetherby's each month to pay the running costs, as well as the training costs, so she gave up and she sold the horse as a brood mare. It had been an enjoyable year, but I can say that if you want to get rid of your money, there's no easier way than to own a racehorse.

Franzi had separated from Charlie and she went back to Switzerland to live in her father's house in Bern. It was a large old Bernese house divided into three flats. Franzi had the top flat and we would sometimes stay with her.

I had seen an advertisement for a short trip to Vienna to visit the Spanish Riding School, and then on to Piber to see the Lipizzaner stud farm. It was a private trip run by Charles Cavendish. We would be staying with Franzi at the time, so I rang him, and he agreed for Jill and I to meet up with them in Vienna. Franzi had never been to Saltzberg, so I decided to take her with us to spend a few days there, before I drove on to Vienna. Franzi would then return to Switzerland by train. She had found a hotel on one of the surrounding hills but when we arrived it was closed.

Driving back down I spotted the Hotel Kobenzl and I enquired about rooms. The woman owner suggested I took their separate annexe suite. This adjoined the hotel and consisted of a large double bedroom with one side equipped with a large desk and armchairs. There were two other bedrooms all en suite, together with a fitness room and indoor pool. It was all very luxurious and it suited us fine.

That night at dinner, madam and all the staff were dressed in Styrian costumes and there was a small orchestra playing. When they brought the menus, I looked across at Franzi and she pointed at me indicating that I look behind me at the high back of my chair. When I did, I saw the little brass plaque that read 'President Nixon'. I looked back across to her chair and there was a similar plaque that read 'Henry Kissinger'.

Later we saw all the photos in the hall of Nixon's visit, and we had been given the rooms that he, his wife and his bodyguard had had stayed in.

At dinner I did my usual thing and I bought the orchestra a drink, and we all enjoyed the occasion.

The next day, we looked around Salzburg and we visited Tomaselli's Tea House, where it's said that you would see every celebrity in the world if you sat there long enough.

After three days, Franzi caught the train back to Bern, and Jill and I enjoyed a few more days before we drove on to Vienna.

We reached the Hotel Central and we booked in. The group who we were to join up with had been delayed and they were expected in time for dinner. We waited in the bar and they finally arrived at nine p.m. and we introduced ourselves to Charles and the others.

Jill did not think that they were very friendly towards us as 'outsiders'.

The door then opened, and a voice said, "Well you never know who you will meet on these holidays."

It was Bernard and Margaret, who we'd met two years before in Seville.

The next day was Sunday and the four of us went to the Stadt Centrum where there were tables and chairs set up around the large patio, outside a large building that contained a restaurant. There was an orchestra playing on the bandstand and the conductor would announce each piece by saying "Meine damen und herren," followed by the name of the music.

I shall never forget the army of waiters gliding around the tables, carrying large silver trays of cakes and pastries, balanced on one hand above their shoulders.

Part of the holiday was a visit to a performance of the Spanish Riding School, in the hall, with its balcony and its chandeliers. The high school routine was impressive, and it was performed to music in their traditional uniforms.

Visiting the stables afterwards we could not help noticing how puffy the stallions' fetlocks were, showing the strain it puts on their joints when performing these feats.

A few days earlier, the border into Czechoslovakia had been opened to allow a few tourists to go beyond the 'Iron Curtain'. Jill and I obtained visas and we took the hydrofoil on the Danube from Vienna to Bratislava.

We were joined by two Americans, and a Spanish couple. There should have been eight of us, but a Dutch couple were refused entry.

When we entered Russian waters, a gunboat escorted us to Bratislava, where we were met by a guide and we were told that we must not stray away from him.

The whole place was filthy. The buses were very old, and they belched out thick diesel smoke and the streets were full of rubbish. The slab-sided apartment blocks were grey and dirty and although I'd been brought up in poverty, this was something else! The only clean building was the Communist Union headquarters and the many statues of Russian victorious soldiers.

The guide took us to a supermarket where the food shelves were empty except for large tins of sausages and dishes of coleslaw. The sports equipment, however, was in plentiful supply, with tennis and skating being prominent. We were taken to a shop that was opened for us, where we were given a meal of some kind of stew. The door was locked behind us, but people began queuing outside, thinking that it would open later.

An hour before we were due to catch the hydrofoil back, the guide said that we could look around, but to be sure to meet him back at the dockside by four-thirty p.m.

Our hotel had given us a packed lunch that Jill produced from her bag. We sat on a wall, eating some rolls, and soon a huddle of children gathered to watch us. They were like the urchins in 'Oliver' and we gave them the apples and the rest of the lunch. Their little faces lit up with delight. After that, we wandered around but everywhere was blocked with barbed wire and notices of 'vstup zakazan' — 'entry forbidden'.

When we got back to Vienna, Bernard said he thought that they would never see us again. Shortly after that, I think the Iron Curtain was closed again.

The group took a coach to visit Graz, but the four of us took my car. I detoured to Yugoslavia, driving through the scenic route of vineyards that criss-crossed the border. We came to a small town where we found a bank to exchange some money, and then we found a small restaurant. We could not understand the menu and I ordered what I thought was chicken, but it turned out to be a kind of white sausage.

After the meal, as we were about to drive off, the village idiot approached us and persisted in trying to help us. Bernard said he thought that he was trying to tell us that we need not have gone all through the countryside, as there was a motorway that would be quicker. I think that he worked for the local sawmills as when I thanked him and we shook hands, he only had two fingers.

Later we visited a market, and to use up our money we saw a stall selling fruit. We gave all the coins to the woman and we indicated that we would like some cherries. We went off, each clutching a large brown paper bag full of them.

***

We arrived in Graz and we booked in at the Palais Hotel Erzherzog. Charlie, (Charles Cavendish) who was sixty-four with his twenty-seven-year-old secretary Nicci, sat with us at dinner that evening, and he said that he was fed up with the others. He was not a man to suffer fools gladly and he was rather like the hotel manager from Fawlty Towers. He asked if we would like to go to the opera the next evening, and we all went to see 'The Magic Flute'.

Afterwards, he took us to a bierkeller where the violin player comes around to the tables. Shortly afterwards, he said that Nicci wanted to go and so they left.

The four of us stayed on, enjoying the atmosphere, and when we left it was pitch black outside.

We did not have a clue where we were, and Margaret said that we should go off to the right. I said that we should go to the left, which we did. It took us over an hour to find the hotel. Had we gone to the right we would have only been ten minutes away.

The following day we all went to Piber to tour the National Lipizzaner Stud farm, and the next day Bernard and Margaret flew home with the group, while Jill and I drove home. I had decided to drive back through Germany and visit the Black Forest.

On the Autobahn, north of Munich my windscreen shattered. I pulled off and I waited for the roadside patrol who arrived and fitted a plastic screen. However, they had knocked out the old windscreen of my Granada and they had pulled off the surrounding rubber and chrome edging, then they screwed it up and threw it on the side of the road.

They said there was a Ford agent at a place called Pfaffenhofen south of Nuremberg, and then they drove off.

Before I continued, I picked up the old rubber and chrome surround and I put it in the boot. It was not long before it started to rain and I then saw that they had fitted the plastic windscreen upside down, with the slots for the wipers at the top.

The next thing it collapsed and blew in, leaving us exposed to the weather; so much for the much-vaunted German engineering.

When we reached Pfaffenhofen we found the Ford garage and they had a windscreen, but they said that they could not fit it without the rubber and the chrome surround. Luckily, I had retrieved this, so they were able to fix the new screen. I only had Swiss francs, but they accepted them as the rate of exchange against the mark was in their favour.

It was dark when we left and drove on. We came to the outskirts of Ulm where we found a small hotel for the night. It seemed to be empty and we booked in and we were shown to our room. It was not what we'd been used to, but any port in a storm as they say.

The toilet was along the corridor and when Jill went to use it, she came back and she told me that there was no lock on the door. I stood outside and I began to take stock of the place. I was in two minds to stay, but as it was only for one night, I decided to put up with it.

Our room had a metal shower cabinet and a wash basin, and when I looked at the skirting boards there were holes all along them. Jill asked what they were, and I told her that they were probably holes where old pipework had been pulled out.

When we came down to dinner, we were the only ones, except for an American sergeant sitting alone at another table. After dinner, he came over and he asked to join us. He was with the US Air Force and he told us that they were billeted there. He said that his unit was made up of recruits from the Southern States and that they had come from farming communities and they weren't very bright. Most of them were hillbillies who could not write their own name. He said that they were all on drugs and that the unit was in a shamble. If the Russians started anything, we would not have a chance.

He was a quietly spoken man and I noticed that he had a bible that he placed on the table. We said goodnight and we went up to our room.

I told Jill that there could be trouble when the airmen came back, and I placed a chest of drawers in front of the bedroom door which also had no lock.

I've never had trouble sleeping, but Jill never slept well. She woke me and she said that there was something in the room. It was all quiet outside, and the airmen had not come back. I put on the light and I saw a rat disappear down one of the holes.

As we lay there through the night, every time we heard a noise, I banged my shoe against the metal shower cabinet.

We got up at five a.m. and I found a woman in the kitchen where I paid her what I thought was enough, and we left. I drove to the Black Forest resort of Baden-Baden where we found a nice café that was open. We had a lovely breakfast and they let us use their washroom facilities. We then headed to France and the Channel port to home.

***

Back then the cross-Channel car ferries were mainly Sealink from Dover to Calais or Folkestone to Boulogne. These short sea crossings took about ninety minutes.

Sealink ran a drivers' club and members had their own lounge and restaurant, overlooking the bow of the ship. It meant that you could sit in comfort and enjoy a meal while crossing. It had waiter service and often when we crossed, there were only one or two other people sharing the spot. It was necessary then to queue at the purser's office for the passport check during the crossing.

I always booked a cabin, so that the purser would come and take our passports for checking, thus saving us the bother. He would also send the steward who would bring us tea and cakes if it was an afternoon sailing. Being in the club, with a cabin booked, also meant that the purser met us when we arrived at the Channel port.

As we drove on, he instructed the Bosun to direct me onto the turntable, so that my car was at the front and we would be the first to drive off. On top of that, it gave you a hefty discount every time you booked. This lasted for quite some time, but in the end, I think that they realised that it lost them money, so they stopped it.

***

One winter's night, crossing in storm force winds to Dunkirk, it was so rough that the ship was rocking, even when it was tied up alongside the quay. This was the boat train, and cars were deck loaded and chained down when it was rough. To drive off meant driving over a hinged steel ramp which swivelled in the middle.

The Bosun stood there, and every time the ship levelled off, he would indicate to you to drive over it. He waved to me, but just as he did the ship lurched and the ramp lifted in the middle and stopped me. He kept beckoning me on, so I put my foot down and we shot off. I was driving a Ford Granada automatic, with a 3-litre engine with lots of torque.

What had happened was that the metal lip in the middle of the ramp had lifted upwards and it had caught against the car's exhaust boxes. The force of my acceleration had pushed them off as the car sped forwards.

As we drove away, the exhaust noise was deafening, the car filled with fumes and it was obvious that we could not drive on. It was four thirty a.m. on a Sunday morning. I saw a garage with lights on and I drove onto the forecourt. There was a Frenchman inside and with Jill's help we made him understand what had happened.

He started up the hydraulic lift, and when the car was lifted, it revealed that both the exhaust boxes were not damaged, but that they had been pushed off the pipes. He refitted them and we drove off to Switzerland.

When I returned home, I wrote to Sealink and I sent them the bill from the garage, claiming reimbursement. They wrote back saying that it was my fault, as the Bosun had said that when my wife had got into the car, that it weighed it down, thus causing insufficient clearance.

I replied that my wife was not an amazon and that she only weighed eight and a half stone. In the end they accepted responsibility and they paid up.

Chapter 16

My accountant in Tonbridge phoned me to say that the Inland Revenue were instigating an enquiry into my tax affairs. I drove up to see him and he explained that the inspector was well known as someone who would never let go until he'd found something. He said that to deal with it would take up a lot of time and be costly. I said nobody knew my affairs better than me, and therefore I would deal with it personally.

In my first eyeball to eyeball with the inspector, he wanted to know a lot about my activities and he then asked what I gave my wife for housekeeping. I told him that if he told me what he gave his wife, I would do likewise.

I appreciated that he had a job to do but I found his attitude offensive. When the interview ended, he said that he would be back in touch.

This went on for several months and then my accountant informed me that the inspector had left, having had a nervous breakdown.

I was then interviewed by another inspector who asked if I would agree to him having access to my bank and my building society accounts. I said that he could contact them, and he later asked me about various deposits. These were perfectly justifiable, and he dropped his enquiries into the matter.

He then called me in one day and he said that on examining my bank account he found that I had written out cheques every week and that I paid myself several hundred pounds each week that I had not declared in my accounts. I let him pursue this line of questioning and then I told him that they were the payments that I had to make every week to the Customs and Excise.

Before I opened for business every Monday, I had to have in my possession a certified certificate to say that I had paid my estimated betting tax for that week in advance. It was the duty that I was obliged to collect for the government, and it was not in my accounts as it was nothing to do with my profit and loss. I saw his face drop, as he obviously thought that he had caught me out.

After that, I wrote to the chief inspector, saying that I had been harassed by them for months and had I been black, or a layabout on benefit, that they would be doing all that they could to help me.

Six weeks later I received a letter from him as follows:

'Dear Mr Saunders.

Thank you for your letter dated 24 October. I apologise for the delay in replying. Unfortunately, Mr Glencross has been transferred and his successor has not yet taken up duty. Your comprehensive statement of your capital position and explanations resolves the enquiries made by this office into your affairs. I am sorry that you feel aggrieved at the need to make these enquiries, but it is incumbent on the inspector to satisfy himself that a taxpayer's returns are correct and to do so, it is frequently necessary to review the whole spectrum of his affairs. I can now agree with your accountant's computations'.

He went on to offer me advice as to my tax position, regarding the Stallions and my intention to begin a stud farm and he enclosed a booklet that he thought might be of assistance.

My accountant was in awe, as he said that they had never had a successful conclusion to a case, and I could work for them (the accountants) any time.

***

Most of the land at Pardlestone sloped and I wanted a large level area where I could school Jubiloso. I decided to build my own all-weather schooling arena, but first I needed to level off a large enough area to construct it.

I knew a young guy with a digger and an earth moving machine and I explained to him what I wanted. He said that it would leave a six-foot bank on one side and a similar drop on the other. I gave him the go ahead and when he'd finished the bank was ten feet high. He left it at an angle of more than forty-five degrees, and as it was clay, when it rained, it caused it to slip down. It meant that I continually had to clear it before it dried, as clay dries like concrete. After that, I let the whole area settle for eighteen months to avoid any sinking later.

When the time came to build the arena, I had two hundred and twenty tons of stone delivered and I spread this over the ground with six-inch land drains to ensure that it would not flood. Next, I had several loads of second-hand railway crossing timbers delivered. I fitted these onto concrete blocks to form a perimeter forming a 40x20 metre rectangle.

Next, I bought rolls of a very tough fibreglass blanket that's called Polyfelt TS that's used in the construction of major highways. This allows water to pass through and it does not rot. I had to overlap this and seal all the edges with a blowlamp. It was now time for the final covering, and I chose a special wood fibre called Dormit. I needed sixty-six tonnes (two hundred cubic metres) to cover the whole area to a depth of nine inches (twenty-three centimetres.). This was delivered by container lorries carrying thirty cubic metres.

The last load was sent on a motorway lorry carrying sixty cubic metres and it got stuck in the bottom of the lane. I knew the director of Kilve Court, Ray Hancock, who rang me to tell me what had happened. The driver said that he had to offload it as he was going on to pick up another load. Kilve Court is a residential school next to the entrance of Pardlestone Lane and Ray agreed to let the driver tip it onto his car park. This was conditional that I then moved it by tractor and trailer as soon as possible.

I don't think he realised what a mountain it would make, and it completely covered the car park like a pyramid, it blocked the entrance to the garages.

It then rained for six weeks and I was unable to shift it. Every time I went by the school to visit our village store, I had to hide my face. Eventually I shifted it and I completed my schooling area and then I began to teach Jubiloso (who we had nicknamed 'Hubi') high school dressage. This is an advanced form of dressage movements.

***

There were a number of women who owned pure bred Spanish mares, and some contacted me. A meeting was set up and with the help of Neil Dougall, it was decided to form a British Andalusian Horse Society. I became a founder member and it was later affiliated to the Spanish society. I started a breeding programme with 'Hubi' at stud. Before I did, I thought that I should have a practice session as this was new to me and the stallion.

John Lamacraft had a little mare that was in season, so I took Hubi over to him. John held the little mare while I had Hubi and I led him up to try the mare. She was obviously in season, but when Hubi mounted her she spun around and shot out through his back legs. After this I decided that I could handle it better at home.

My neighbour, Edré McElwee, herself an experienced horsewoman, acted as my stud groom holding the mares. After 'trying' them she held the mares while I led Hubi up to do the business. This worked well and it is a better method rather than involving too many people that only get in the way.

We had kept in touch with Bernard and Margaret and they came down quite regularly to stay with us in the annexe. Bernard was a very good rider and he used to enjoy riding Hubi in training sessions. Margaret had her own horse, but she was wanting to find a replacement. I found her an Anglo Arab mare and she bought it.

Margaret was not ready to have the mare back in Surrey, so it was arranged that I would keep the mare for her and breed a foal for myself. This was a very successful cross resulting in a Hispano Anglo-Arab that I named Luchador. The reason for this name is that in Spanish it means a fighter or a struggler who never gives up.

Back then ultrasound scans were not available, and it was left to you, or the Vet's judgement as to whether the mare was in foal. When the time got near, I said to Jill that I did not think that the mare was in foal, as she had only come into heat once and received service.

She was out in the paddock and that night there was a violent thunderstorm. I went out early to check on her and I could not see her anywhere. Then I spotted her standing by the far hedge, and as I approached, I first saw the discarded placenta on the ground.

I then saw this shivering little foal standing next to her. I led the mare back to her box with the little foal staggering along behind. Once inside the foal tried to suckle but the mare refused and she became very aggressive, to the point of being dangerous to all concerned in the confines of the box.

I should explain that it is essential that a foal receives its mother's milk at the start, as it contains the vital colostrum for its immunity. Without it, the foal cannot begin to produce its own immune system. The mare had given birth some nine days less than a full term and her milk had not quite come down. It took a lot of effort to get her to let the foal suckle as he would not stop trying. Once successful, he would then punch her udder, nearly lifting her off her feet.

I left 'Luchador' with the mare for nine months before weaning him off. He then grew into a handsome grey gelding of sixteen hands.

Bernard was down with us when it was time for breaking 'Luke' to the saddle. I'd left this for some time as a horse's bones are not properly set until they're five or six years old.

The fact that racehorses are broken and ridden from the age of two, is not in the horse's interest. It's purely financial and this is the reason why many break down.

We took 'Luke' up to the schooling arena and I introduced the saddle. He accepted this without fuss, and he allowed me to mount. No sooner had I taken up the reins when he began to buck and behave like a rodeo horse.

Unable to dislodge me, he threw himself down onto the ground, trapping my leg under him. Struggling to get up he proceeded to kick me in the back and Margaret ran across, thinking that he had killed me. I lay there laughing as I saw the funny side of it.

When we tried again, Bernard said he thought that I was too heavy for a first-time mounting, and that he should try. When he mounted Luke immediately bucked and he threw Bernard straight over his back. I'll always remember Bernard's long legs disappearing as he flew backwards through the air.

I tried again and this time it was successful. When I took Luke back to his box and removed the bridle, one of his molar milk teeth dropped into my hand. These are pushed out by the eruption of the permanent teeth and this had been the reason for his behaviour. I still have the tooth on the shelf in the store.

The society members were sending their mares to me, and with Jill's and Edré's help I continued with the breeding programme.

Jill's younger sister Jacie, her husband Mick and their son Grant would come down for holidays, and Grant would come and stay during his school holidays. He enjoyed working with his grandfather Len in the garden and he would help me with the various jobs about the place.

I had a foal that I'd bred from a friend's mare and they were turned out together. The mares name was Belle and as the sire was Jubiloso, I named her Jezabelle. She was high-spirited and she refused to be caught. I needed to check her over, so Grant and I went to catch her.

I'd made a metal hook fixed to a pole, rather like a shepherd's crook. There was a wooden shed one end of the paddock about six feet from the hedge, and I told Grant to chase the mare and the foal and that I would stand behind the shed and hook Jezabelle as they came around.

When they cantered past, I leaped out and I hooked the foal, but she was stronger than I thought. She galloped off, with me running behind hanging on. As she gained on me, I gradually lost my balance, and the hook broke and sent me flying. I landed flat on my face and I slithered along the ground still gripping the pole.

Grant ran over to me and said, "Are you all right Uncle?"

I could see that he had difficulty not to burst out laughing.

It must have looked like one of those scenes from 'You've Been Framed'. I was okay and we both had a good laugh. Eventually I caught the foal and she was fine.

***

Jill and I went to the Devon County show to buy some chickens. We had kept hens for some time but we wanted some 'Silkies'. Jill's first purchase had been a little bantam. When she brought it home and she told her father that she'd bought a young bird, he took one look and he said that she'd been done.

Len had kept chickens for years and he knew how to tell their age by the scales on their legs. We called it 'the old girl'.

One winter, we had set off for Switzerland in the snow and when I reached the bottom of the lane, all the traffic was stuck. I had chains, but it was no good as the road was blocked, so I drove back home.

When I arrived, a fox had dug his way into the chicken run and it had killed all twenty-seven of them. There was blood and dead chickens everywhere. Jill was very upset, and she said that we've lost the old girl.

Shortly afterwards, we looked up and there she was perched on top of the stable roof. This little bantam was a good mother for raising chicks, and although she was tiny, we would put five duck eggs under her, and she would hatch and raise them.

She eventually went blind, and although she had been an aggressive mother, seeing off the other chickens; she was now blind and they would attack her.

We kept her separate, and during the day we let her out into the garden. We had a ginger stable cat called Toasty who befriended the little bantam. Sometimes we would see them together with the bantam standing next to Toasty, propped up against her. It was as if the cat protected her from harm.

One morning I went to let her out and I found that she had died from natural causes. I do not know how old she was, but we had her for seventeen years. The Vet said that it must be a record.

At the Devon Show, Jill spotted a stand with a little Honda pick-up truck. It took her fancy and I asked the salesman about it. I wanted to know what engine it had, but he said don't worry about that. He told us to get in and when we squeezed into the front with him, he drove us around the show grounds. Jill fell in love with it, so I bought it for her.

It proved to be a brilliant vehicle. It was a half-ton pick-up with a 354cc air cooled engine mounted on the back axle. Top speed was fifty-five miles per hour and it had an old type non-synchromesh gearbox. This meant that to change gear smoothly, it was necessary to release and re-engage the clutch at the same time. This was easy for me as most of the army vehicles had this type of gearbox and I'd been taught this method. I showed Jill how to do it and she soon got the hang of it.

It was very useful, and Jill would go off to the feed merchants for supplies, and I would use it for haymaking. Grant was only about thirteen years old when I taught him to drive in it. I even went up to Kent to bring back furniture, driving it there and back nearly four hundred miles in one day. Jill loved it and she drove it everywhere. It was a difficult vehicle to work on when something went wrong, but Jack Neal and I kept it going for her for twenty-five years.

Since the early years at Pardlestone, when we were living the 'Good Life' and enjoying being self-sufficient, we had always kept chickens and ducks. Len had shown me how to humanely kill a chicken by a quick upwards twist of its neck. When the Silkies multiplied, I killed a cock bird for the table.

This variety of poultry have black skins although their flesh is white. The trouble was that when you ate them, you first had to peel away the black skin, and it was like eating a chicken in a rubber wet suit. I gave up on them and I sold any surplus. We kept Aylesbury ducks and from time to time I would kill one for dinner. The trouble was that when I held it up to be poleaxed it would twist its head up and look at me. I did not have the heart to kill them, so their numbers increased.

One morning I was in the bath when Jill's mother shouted upstairs that a fox was after the ducks. I jumped out, scrambled into a pair of pants, grabbed my shotgun and I ran outside. The fox had caught one and he was running up the drive. Before I could do anything, he saw me, and he dropped the duck. When I picked it up it was unhurt as the down beneath its feathers had protected it.

***

I sunk an old cast iron bath into the ground, and I filled it with water to make a pond for them. The trouble was that it did not have running water and it would quickly become stagnant and stink. I was continually emptying it and filling it with fresh water. Ducks, unlike chickens, lay their eggs anywhere and they would often be in the bottom of the bath when I emptied it. I threw these away but the fresh duck eggs we sold.

One morning I rode Hubi up to the schooling arena, when I heard something squeaking. Looking down there was a tiny little yellow duckling running along the path. I dismounted and I picked it up and I took it back with me. I could then hear similar noises coming from under the barn. When I built it, I had put a raised floor to keep the hay off the ground. There was a gap underneath about a foot high.

Getting a torch, I could see a duck nesting over in the far corner. Jill came and we agreed that if we left it there that the fox would get it. I crawled underneath and I grabbed the duck and there were eight little yellow balls of fluff under her.

We rescued them all and we put them in the duck house. Later we enjoyed watching them all swimming around the pond.

One of them was deformed and had one wing on top of its back. It grew into a large drake and because of its deformity it reminded me of the Hunchback of Notre Dame, so we called him Quasimodo. He was the randiest drake I'd ever known. He would pin the ducks to the ground and he would rape them unmercifully. Their squeals could be heard all over the garden, so in the end I did him in.

Jill and I went on a fortnight's walking holiday and we left her cousin Ron and his wife in charge. When we returned, I noticed a fishing net in the feed store. I asked Ron what it was, and he said that he used it to fish out the duck eggs from the pond. He had not changed the water and it was as black as ink.

I said, "You didn't sell them did you Ron?"

Looking sheepish he replied, "No."

I was relieved that when I read the local newspaper that there was no report of any mysterious deaths in the village.

***

My father never remarried, but he lived with Olive, the woman in the shop in Vale Road, until they both retired to a council flat at the other end of town. Her health failed and she went into a nursing home. He would visit her every day, catching three buses each way. When she died, I drove up from Somerset to be with him for the funeral. When I got there, he told me that he had gout in his right foot and that he could not get his shoe on. The next day, when I collected him, I found that he'd cut the back of his shoe off so that he could slip his foot into it.

The funeral was at Mayfield church and when we came outside to follow the coffin to the grave, I helped him along as he had difficulty

211

walking. With the coffin in front of us, and all the other mourners behind, we led the procession. It was down through grass paths with tall hedges each side, rather like a maze.

Halfway down, he suddenly said, "Hang on, I've lost my bloody shoe."

Looking down, I could see it stuck in the mud. I retrieved it and we set off again and I could see the funny side of it and I could not stop laughing. My shoulders shook and the people behind must have hopefully thought that I was sobbing.

The next thing, the coffin turned a bend, and by the time we got there it had disappeared. I did not know which way to go, and by the time we got to the graveside the service was over.

When he got back to the car, he said, "I'm knackered."

In all the years that I lived in Somerset he would never come and visit. He continued to live in his little flat and I rang him every morning and evening. He used to catch the bus to town to do his shopping.

On several occasions when I phoned him, he would complain to me that a woman with an arse so big that she occupied two seats, was following him home. He said that he'd tried to dodge her but, "The bloody woman's always there."

When I visited him later, I found out that she was in the flat next to him, just along the corridor.

***

He used to complain about the schoolboys' behaviour on the buses and he said that they would never give up their seat to a woman.

One day on a crowded bus, he gave up his seat and on standing up, one of the boys said, "You're standing on my foot."

To which he replied, "It's a pity it's not your bloody head."

He had always been very independent and that had not lessened with old age.

One night when I phoned him, he did not answer, so I phoned the warden. She said that she would go and check and when she phoned me back, she told me that he was sitting in his chair but that he had died. He'd given up smoking at the age of eighty. The death certificate said that he had suffered from Chronic Obstructive Pulmonary Disease for twenty years. He was ninety-two.

When I sorted out his things, in his little desk was a wallet. In it there was a photo of my mother, one of her with me as a child holding our little dog Chum, and a photo of Ward Bond the actor. His father would never have his photo taken, but when younger he had a noticeable likeness to the actor.

I could not help but to think that although he had never been able to show his emotions, that he must have felt more deeply towards us than I'd imagined.

***

I'd bought a six-acre field in the lane and I built a large field shelter and a hay barn. A very large feral cat made its home there.

One day as I was feeding the horses, I saw a tiny kitten under the manger. It was almost dead, and Jill said that I should put it out of its misery. I thought that it deserved a chance, so she helped me feed it milk with a small syringe and we gradually nursed it back to health.

When it was old enough, I took it back to live with its mother. I did not want them both breeding litters there, so I arranged for the RSPCA to come and catch the mother so that I could take them to be spayed.

He turned up with a cage, but he had no idea how to do it, so I told him to leave me the cage and that I would do it. I got a smelly kipper and I put it inside the cage and placed it in the hay barn. Before long I heard the door, spring shut, and the cat was inside. I took them both to the Vet and when I returned them, they continued to live there together.

This kept the barn free from any vermin. The kitten grew into a lovely tabby cat and she was very friendly. I named her Misty. She got to know the times when I fed the horses, and when I also took a tin of cat food. She would be waiting at the gate and she would run up behind me into the barn. She would then make a fuss of me until I opened the tin.

The mother would wait at a distance and she would not feed until she saw me leaving.

One day Misty was missing, and I never saw her for three weeks. When she came back, she was thin and in a poor condition. She soon grew back to health and she continued living there. I wondered if a holiday maker had seen her and taken her home with them, and she'd then found her way back home again.

***

A racing pigeon turned up on the roof of our stables. It remained for several days, so I caught it and I took its number off the ring on its leg. I rang the association, but I was told that it would not be any good to race anymore, and that they did not want it back.

I said to Jill that we would take it to Bridgwater and then set it free so that it could find its way home from there. We parked the car and I threw it into the air expecting to see it fly away home.

Instead of flying it just fell straight back onto the road. I said that we'd leave it and go shopping. When we got to the pedestrian crossing, I looked behind and it had followed us. Wherever we went it walked behind us. I took it back to the car and I left it inside while we did the shopping.

On leaving Bridgwater, I left it in the car park, and I drove home, thinking that we'd finally lost it. As I drove in, there it was sitting on the stable roof.

Jill's sister, Molly, and her husband came to stay and when they went back to Kent, I got them to take it and release it on Salisbury Plain. I thought that this might be another ley line that could re-orientate it. I guess it worked as it never returned.

Chapter 17

Despite being dyslexic as a child, I had always had an aptitude for writing. During the time of our Swiss skiing holidays, I had written a novel about a middle-aged Englishman who gets caught up with a smuggling ring in the Alps. He meets and teams up with a young attractive CIA agent and it results in a James Bond-like adventure. I had submitted it to a literary agent and his review was that it was not a masterpiece but that it was good enough to grace the W.H. Smith stands at the airports.

Franzi had introduced us to the village of Schönried, a very good skiing region above Gstaad. We first stayed at the Bahnhof Hotel that was run by the Kernen family. Their small son Bruno would sometimes serve us our breakfast. He later became World Downhill Skiing Champion and he won many races for Switzerland.

Later, we rented an apartment there for many years. On winter days when we were not skiing, we would walk to Gstaad. On the way we would pass the chalet owned by Richard Burton and Elizabeth Taylor. We saw her one-day shopping in the CO-OP. Dressed in a fur coat with a headscarf and no screen make up; you would not have given her a second glance.

Other film stars were often seen in Gstaad when they stayed at the Palace Hotel. In nearby Château d'Oex, David Niven had a chalet. He could often be seen skiing, and he always wore knee length navy blue trousers buckled below the knee, and long red socks.

One day I was skiing on the Eggli when we almost collided. We both stopped and he said something, but it was not very complimentary.

Another village there called Rougemont had a little restaurant called 'du Cerf'. It specialised in cheese fondue and it was a little old wooden building. The little dining room only had three or four tables. It can still be found on the internet, but it's been enlarged and modernised now.

Jill and I went there for lunch one day and we were the only ones there. Jill sat down while I went off to the toilet. When I came back there was another couple with two children sitting at the next table.

The man had his back to Jill, and she leant across to me and whispered, "English."

I mouthed back the words, "David Niven."

He was with his wife Hjordis and their two children. The children were trying to persuade him to take them skating. I'd read that 'Cubby' Broccoli the producer of the James Bond films was looking for his next story, so when I returned to England I wrote to David Niven, saying that we'd met on the Eggli, leaving out the near collision.

I explained about my book and I asked if he would be interested in the story as a possible film in which he might star.

He wrote back to say that unfortunately he had no influence when it came to Broccoli or any other producers, but would I send him the galleys (advance reading copies).

My novel was not published so that ended it. However, I thought that it was very good of him to take the time and trouble to bother with an unknown and show interest. After a later letter to him, his secretary replied saying that he was unwell. Two years later he died from motor neurone disease. He was buried in the small churchyard in Château-d'Oex and when Jill and I returned the next year, we visited the graveside.

***

My next attempt at authorship was after I'd bought the stallions, when I wrote about the history of the Andalusian horse and my experience of bringing them to England. The manuscript was finished, but I had not thought much about publishing it as I was too busy with other things.

One morning I helped Jill do the washing up and she had the radio on. It was 'Women's Hour' and they were interviewing a publisher. It was another 'Fickle Finger of Fate' moment.

The publisher was Ian Morley-Clarke and he lived in Speldhurst near Tunbridge Wells. I was still commuting, and when I went back, I phoned him, and I told him about the horse book that I'd written. He asked to see the manuscript and I arranged to go and see him.

He was very impressed, and he said that he would have no trouble to find a backer who would produce it. Two weeks later, he phoned to tell me that although they had liked the book and thought that it was well written, they thought that the horse was relatively unknown here and it would not generate enough sales.

However, they wanted to know if I had any other ideas. I had not given any thought to another book, but I was not going to let this opportunity pass, so I said that I had. Ian then asked me to produce a synopsis and send it to him.

I came up with the idea for a series of horse books called 'HORSEKEEPING' and under that title the first book was 'Ownership, Stabling and Feeding' that was first published in 1982.

My next book was 'Management, Ailments & Injuries'. My vets were West, Carter and Philips who had a teaching practice in Minehead. George Carter was a surgeon, specialising in horse ailments and diseases. He had a large house in Minehead, and he had built the surgery in the grounds, with a separate operating theatre. Because of my stallions, we all became good friends and George and his wife would often come to us for dinner.

I became very interested in his work and he invited me to witness the operations and to film them. Philip Browne was the anaesthetist and the three of us would go into the operating room with a horse. Everywhere was padded, walls and floor alike, with thick rubber covered mattresses that had been specially made to prevent injury to the horse.

The operating table was sunk into the floor and it was operated hydraulically from the outside. Standing on these bouncy mattresses was not easy, especially when the horse walked on them.

George would lead the horse in and Philip would inject a knockout drug. This was fatal to humans and there had been cases where a vet had jabbed himself when the horse moved and had died almost immediately. An antidote was therefore always kept at hand.

Horses weigh between half and three quarters of a ton and when they are drugged, they stagger about before they fall. This meant that we had to be aware of it falling, so as not to have it fall on top of us as there

217

was not much room. The trick was to get it to fall onto the mattress where the operating table was. If it was not quite right, George would take its back legs, Philip the front legs and me holding its tail, and we would drag it into position.

With the horse in place, the table would be raised, and Philip would insert his apparatus down its throat and administer the anaesthetic. George would then commence the operation and I would film it with an old Russian camera that Jack Neal had lent me. The lenses were good, but it was cumbersome and difficult to focus.

I later bought a Minolta with automatic focusing for close ups. George would move over to let me film right in and he would explain the procedure to me.

Sometimes Jeff Lane, the teaching professor from Bristol University would come down to show George the latest techniques. I worked with them for eighteen months and then I wrote the book.

After that I obtained freelance contracts with several horse magazines to provide articles, and I also supplied them with photos for their other contributors.

My third book was 'Riding and Training' and all three books were published by Frederick Muller Limited of London.

My fourth book was 'Small Scale Breeding' and it was published by Sterling Publishing New York. One day I had a telephone call from Burton Hobson their President, to say that he had the initial five thousand and that he had sent my advance, but he had not received the full quota. He asked what was going on, but I told him that I was not aware of this.

The producers in England were The Baton Press and I knew their director Ray Green, so I rang him. He told me that they had sunk a lot of money into producing a religious book that questioned the origins of Christianity but they had been receiving death threats, so they had pulled out and had gone into liquidation. He said that I should come and see him to collect anything that was mine by copyright.

When I searched through his desk, I found a letter from a Spanish Literary Agent in Barcelona. My book had been taken to the annual book fair in Frankfurt where it had been seen by Julio Yanez, and he had written to say that he thought he knew of a Spanish publisher who would like to produce a Spanish edition.

Ray Green had not passed this on to me and he said that he'd forgotten about it. I enquired as to my advance that Burton Hobson had forwarded to him, and he told me that it was all in the hands of the liquidator.

I contacted them and I explained that the money had been sent to me via the producers and therefore I should receive it. I was told that it was included in what assets they'd confiscated, and as the tax man had first claim there was nothing left to pay me.

I thought this unjust, but to pursue it was pointless as this was the law and to challenge it would have been too costly.

Consequently, I lost it all. However, I contacted the agent in Barcelona and the outcome was a contract with Hispano Europea who published the book worldwide in Spanish, and it remained on their list for twenty years.

***

I sold our Tonbridge house in 1984 and in 1989 I sold the bookmaking business. Den had wanted to retire at sixty, but he had hung on for three years so that I could benefit from tax relief on the sale when I reached sixty. It was at the time when the major firms were expanding their betting shop chains and Coral and several other firms showed interest in my Paddock Wood office.

A former Ladbrokes financial adviser was working for Richard Jennings who owned chains in London and Essex and he was seeking to expand into Kent. He said it needed eight shops to make it viable and that mine would be ideal as the hub. We concluded a deal, and in January 1990 I went with him to the magistrates' court in Tunbridge Wells to get the licence transferred. There was no need to, but I wore my regimental tie, as it was to be my last court appearance.

My solicitor arranged the payment, and it gave me great pleasure to give Den a cheque for the half that he truly deserved for his efforts in helping to make the business a success. I had got out just in time, as not long after that the major firms began disposing of their shops, as there were too many competing with each other.

***

I continued to ride 'Hubi', and 'Luke' had trained on to a competent level. However, I was in my sixties and I was beginning to wonder if it was time to give up riding and do something else.

Never in all my life, whether riding, skiing or motorcycling, had I worn a hard hat or any protective clothing. This must be stupid, and I would always advise others not to be so foolhardy.

For me, however, it offered the uninhibited freedom and the adrenalin rush, that is muffled by a helmet.

I could never decide which was the greatest thrill, rushing almost uncontrolled downhill on a pair of skis, or galloping at thirty-five miles per hour, on top of the half ton of muscle, bone and blood of a good horse. There is no doubt that if there had been the opportunities that young people have today, when I was young, I would have found more excitement.

'Hubi' was almost twenty years old and his legs began to fail. He would get down in his box and struggle to get up. Some nights Jill would wake me and say that she could hear him kicking the side of his box. I would dress and go to his box to find him cast. This is when the horse rolls against the side of the box and cannot get up. I would help him up and stay with him until he recovered.

One day he staggered to get up and he fell forwards striking his head on the manger. George, my Vet, said that there was nothing to be done and that I should think about having him put down.

If you undertake to keep animals, you are responsible for their wellbeing, and you have a duty not to let them suffer. I soon realised that the Vet had been right, and I arranged for the Exmoor Hunt to come and dispatch him.

After it was done, they loaded his body onto a trailer, and they drove off down the drive. I watched them disappear through the gate, I then stood there, and I sobbed like a child.

Jubiloso's life ended outside his box in familiar surroundings, as I stood with him in the morning sunlight of a bright December day. He knew no pain or fear, as death came instantaneously. I must say that it was the most heart-breaking thing I had ever done. He'd been part of my life for many years and we had shared a mutual respect for one another. The British Andalusian Horse Society published his photo on the cover of their winter magazine, with a tribute inside and a poem that I wrote:

REQUIEM TO HUBI

'A noble horse this Spanish grey.
A gentleman in every way.
When young he was so proud yet kind.
Never he with spiteful mind.
He didn't crave for power or fame
work and servitude was his game
And in old age, still bright of eye
He didn't know he had to die
No longer could he roll or sleep
with crippled back and legs so weak
I hoped that he would understand,
as he took the apple from my hand,
I led him to a quiet spot
and stood with him as he was shot.

***

Nicky Stevens, a lady farmer, had always wanted to own an Andalusian and when she saw Luke, she asked me if I would consider selling him to her. She was an experienced horsewoman and I knew that she would give him a good home, so I agreed. But I would not sell him to her unless she would take Jezabelle as well, as they had always been together.

I said that I was willing to let her have the mare for nothing, to keep the two of them from being separated. She agreed, and she housed them next to each other in two special horseboxes. I visited them from time to time, and sometimes I watched her when she rode 'Luke' in equestrian events.

***

A couple from Yorkshire, Elizabeth and Peter Mansbridge, would come each Spring and stay in the annexe. They were both keen gardeners and very knowledgeable. Jill and I began to go with them down to Cornwall to visit the National Trust, and other gardens open to the public.

I had never seen such wonderful plants, especially the Rhododendrons and the Magnolias. I was smitten and I told Jill that I would create a garden for our old age.

We began travelling all over the south of England to specialist growers and nurseries, and I spent a small fortune obtaining rare and unusual species. I was most interested in trees and shrubs, and our Yorkshire friends said that they considered me to be a plants man, rather than a gardener.

I landscaped a large part of our garden, and with Jill's help, I cleared overgrown waste ground to develop the site and transform it into a beautiful garden. The soil for growing Rhododendrons must be slightly acid. I tested mine and I found some acid parts, but it was slightly alkaline in other parts.

A building site in the village was clearing the soil from an old forge, that had made the soil very acid. I arranged for several trailer loads and I spread it over where I planted. The planting took about three years before it was completed. Some species can take fifteen years before they flower, and Jill and I enjoyed many years watching the garden mature.

People used to ask us how we managed to maintain it by ourselves, and I would tell them that it looked after itself. I would then add, providing you work on it every day. Jill loved it and she was always keen to be working in it.

Most of the flowering shrubs are at their best in Springtime when there is a wonderful display. But I also included those trees and shrubs that display autumn colours, so that we get another period later in the year to create a picture.

Pardlestone is a special place, and we always enjoyed having good neighbours and a friendly community. In summer, we would often barbecue together and visit one another socially from time to time.

Our original idea of 'The Good Life' had developed over the years and Jill and I were as happy as any couple could be, enjoying the home and the garden that we had created.

Chapter 18

Another 'Fickle Finger of Fate' moment came, that was to shatter my life. We'd enjoyed a wonderful Spring together, and the garden had never looked better. Grant and Richard, his partner, were staying with us in the annexe, and we'd had a memorable time together.

Jill suffered a sudden fatal accident and she died the following morning in hospital.

I'd always considered myself to be a tough character able to cope with anything that life threw at me, but this devastated me. Grant and Richard, and later Jill's younger sister Jacie, got me through it.

Richard made all the arrangements for Jill's funeral. We'd both always said that we would want this to be without fuss, and not being religious, a simple humanist ceremony was arranged. Grant, being an accountant and a financial consultant, dealt with all the paperwork. I shall always be indebted to them for their support.

Jill had been a wonderful, unselfish, caring person, who had always supported me in everything that I did. We had trusted each other completely, and we never had any secrets from each other. We had been lovers, soulmates and friends for more than sixty-two years and she was a part of me.

She suffered from arthritis for many years, and although her fingers were very painful, she never ever complained, and she never let it prevent her from working in her beloved garden. I always tried to do my best for her, and every day we would sit at lunch and clink glasses and say how lucky we were.

There isn't a day that passes when I do not think about her, and I miss her greatly. When I'm in the garden I think of her there with her old bucket and tools and I feel her presence. No words can adequately express the bond that we had but looking back and comparing what we had to what most people get from life, I can only say, 'How Lucky Can You Get'.

Epilogue

The following year, Grant and Richard moved to Pardlestone to share the property with me. They completely renovated and modernised the annexe to make it their home.

They both love the garden and Richard is keen to develop his own version of 'The Good Life' by creating a new vegetable garden. Grant has semi-retired from his business, so as to leave him more time for the garden.

It is gratifying for me to know, that when my time comes to finally leave Pardlestone, the legacy that Jill and I created will continue in our absence.

Poverty didn't prevent my mother from dressing me nicely as a child.
She made this velvet suit for this portrait photo.

Len's pride and joy, the Vauxhall VX90.

My Sunbeam Rapier rally equipped, next to the E Type Jaguar.

Ken and me about to commence a game of jokari on the sands at
Eastbourne.

The barn I converted in Somerset and the stables that enabled me to set
up the stud with my stallions.

Always the clown, Jack Wells removed his shoes and stood in a hole for this photo.

Charlie and Franzi Tuerlinckx, who we met in Riederalp, Switzerland.

Me and Jill with the lace up boots and long skis of the 1960s.

Jill with her original ski bike that came from Grindlewald, Switzerland.

Me with Fredi, 18hh, at the Swiss Olympic Equestrian Centre, Finsterhennon.

A 1960s view of Monaco.

The palace guards looking like toy soldiers.

Paco displays the two stallions at Finca Mahaloba in Seville.

At home in Somerset.

Jean helping Jill in the vineyard.

Me treading the grapes, with Jack Neal helping and his wife looking on.